ation

triumph

SHARP

FINCH PUBLISHING
SYDNEY

Transformation: Turning tragedy into triumph

First published in 2016 in Australia and New Zealand by Finch Publishing Pty Limited,
ABN 49 057 285 248, Suite 2207, 4 Daydream Street, Warriewood, NSW, 2102, Australia.

16   8 7 6 5 4 3 2 1

There is a National Library of Australia Cataloguing-in-Publication entry available at the
National Library.

Edited by Jenny Scepanovic
Editorial assistance by Megan English
Text typeset by Vicki McAuley
Cover design by Jo Hunt
Printed by Griffin Press

Reproduction and communication for educational purposes

The paper used to produce this book is a natural, recyclable product made from wood grown in
sustainable plantation forests. The manufacturing processes conform to Australian environmental
regulations.

Finch titles can be viewed and purchased at **www.finch.com.au**

Contents

This book is dedicated to all those wonderful people who have supported, and continue to support, others in times of need.

My support network is my incredible wife and my rapidly maturing and increasing incredible children. Before them, it was my parents who provided endless and unconditional love, as well as my brother and sister who were, in their own ways, always there for me.

And to all of you who are reading this, whether you have experienced a form of trauma first-hand or have supported someone who has, thank you for reading, thank you for spreading the word and helping more people seek the support they need.

Introduction

I love what I do. I'm not saying every single minute or every single day is 100 per cent perfect, but more often than not I derive enormous satisfaction from finding creative ways to help clients (individuals and organisations) overcome adversity, move beyond depression and stress, and create more happiness and success in their lives.

I also love the variety of what I do. One day I might be sitting in a room, having one-on-one coaching or therapy sessions with individuals. Another day I could be writing, or developing a new workplace program proposal. And on yet another day I could be speaking at a conference or within the context of a workplace or organisational event to several hundred or even several thousand people.

No two days are ever the same, and I like it like that.

One particular aspect of all the various activities from which I derive pleasure is meeting amazing and inspirational people. For a variety of reasons, in a range of different settings, I constantly find myself meeting some of the most courageous, resilient, happy, successful, mind-bogglingly creative and entrepreneurial people. And I love it! I love talking to them, listening to their stories and most importantly, learning from them.

Which is where the idea for this book came from.

One day I was reflecting on a thoroughly interesting and inspiring meeting I'd just had and I began to think of all the other amazing people I'd met over the years who in different ways had also been interesting and inspiring.

Now some of these people had already written and told their stories; and all of them (to a greater or lesser extent) are already publicly known for what they've achieved. But it struck me that bringing them all together in one place might be a wonderfully useful resource.

I envisaged an easy-to-read and accessible book, within which a range of different stories were told by a range of different people; different stories in different voices with many different lessons to be learnt – all in the one place. This way, I thought, people would be able to take different things from different parts of the book and ultimately benefit in different ways.

And here we have it: eleven chapters from eleven amazing people with eleven remarkable stories. Each and every one of their stories is well worth reading. They all contain incredibly valuable life lessons, even for those of us who might not have faced exactly the same challenges or who might not share their passions. But with a little thought and reflection we can all take something from their experiences that will, indubitably, prove useful in some way in our own lives.

I'm so proud of this book and so excited for you and many others to read it because it brings together such a wide range of people and issues. It also raises and asks a diverse range of questions. Accordingly, it offers so much to those who read it with an open mind and a willingness to listen and learn; to reflect and change; to become who we might be thanks to them, their generosity and, in some cases, courage in sharing their personal stories.

So how does it work?

Well, it doesn't work; you do. That is, you decide how you want to read it and what you want to take from it.

You can read it front to back, although please note that there's not necessarily any particular order of the chapters. Alternatively, you can dip in and out of different chapters randomly or based on your assumptions about which ones might be most relevant to you. But do remember that these are assumptions! I guarantee you'll be surprised by some of the contributors and their stories and their possible relevance to you and your life, despite what might at first appear to be a lack of connection. So please consider reading ALL the chapters, even if not in order.

And as you do proceed, I very strongly recommend that you do more than just read. I encourage you to take notes, develop plans, set goals and generally think of ways you can use this book to create an even better life for yourself – and possibly an even better world for everyone around you. To assist with this I offer a professional and independent perspective at the end of each chapter, teasing out what I believe to be the most important aspects and lessons. I also provide you with action steps and recommendations regarding strategies that you can then implement in your own life with a view to enjoying more happiness and success.

At the risk of repeating myself, remember that for this book to work, YOU need to work. It's certainly true, to some extent, that 'it's the thought that counts'; but it's also very much true that 'actions speak louder than words'. So learn from these eleven incredible people, take action, make changes and find ways to keep going in the direction you want and need to go in order to thrive and flourish!

Bouncing forward

Sam Cawthorn

Sam's incredible story is so inspiring: his resilience and the success he's had in not just surviving, but thriving. In October 2006 Sam's life changed forever when he was involved in a major car accident where he was pronounced dead. He was thankfully resuscitated, but his right arm was amputated and he was left with a permanent disability in his right leg. He has gone on to write six books and become a leading motivational speaker as well as founding a charity devoted to helping children with disabilities in developing countries. He is the 2015 Young Australian of the Year.

Pain is inevitable; misery is optional.

It was a cold afternoon and you could smell spring in the air. Winter had passed but sitting there alone in the shredded car with the entire right side of the car ripped off and my bones and flesh exposed to the afternoon sun, I felt cold. I was shivering and sweating at the same time. I was feeling pulses of shivers all over my body that I could not control. Was I going to die? I kept asking myself, is this it? Was this the last ever moment of my life right here? I thought about my two little girls, I thought about how they could comprehend the magnitude of what happened to their daddy. I thought about my wife, not knowing if I would ever see her again.

Flashes of images rushed through my mind: a single mother, fatherless children, a funeral. I was so sad, not just from the pain but because I was thinking about everything. My mind was going at warp speed – what life meant, my friends, my family and my whole life up until now. What could I have done differently? What could I have done better? Why didn't I try more? Why couldn't I have not taken life for granted too much? Was this really happening? Was this the end? Are these really the last breaths I would ever take?

No, Sam, stop thinking these thoughts. Fight, FIGHT, there is still hope …

The pain was taking away every freedom I had from my body. My lungs were fighting for every ounce of air they could get. My eyelids felt like a ton of bricks. I just wanted to close them and go to sleep. 'SAM, SAM, STAY AWAKE FOR US!' my rescuers yelled. 'SAM, YOU CAN DO IT, HOLD ON!'

I felt an overwhelming fear and darkness suffocate everything that life represented. I was yelling to God to save me. I was telling my rescuers my wife's number so they could call her and I could say goodbye. The meaning of life and death was suddenly real, so real. Life was becoming no more. 'WHAT IS HAPPENING?' I yelled as tears ran down my face. 'RING MY WIFE. TELL HER I LOVE HER!'

My car had been torn and ripped to shreds on the main highway between Devonport and Launceston, Tasmania.

Australia. It was a large highway, and people started to crowd around. As the silhouettes started to yell, that was when I knew it was serious.

There are pivotal moments within moments, game-changing moments in time – the Greeks called them kairos moments. For some, these moments are so significant that they immediately fracture life, ripping it forever into two parts – everything before, and everything after.

For me, my kairos moment occurred just after 3 pm on 3 October 2006. The day had started normally enough. I woke up early as usual, assisted by my eldest daughter Emelia, who was three and a half at the time. As the house stirred into life Milly (as we affectionately call her) left my wife Kate and I, and went to wake up her little sister Ebony who was just fifteen months old. The girls watched some cartoons as Kate prepared their breakfast and I got ready for work. It has always been a Cawthorn family tradition to sit down at the table together, eat breakfast and discuss our plans for the day. After breakfast the girls and I put some loud music on and danced around the living room together. I would throw each one up in the air and catch them as they squealed and giggled with delight. I thought to myself how lucky I was and what a great way to start the day.

At the time I was working as an industry adviser on young people's trends and careers, like a youth futurist, an initiative funded by the Australian Federal Government. I'd only been in the job a few months but I loved it. I was just 26 years old, I had a big job, a good salary and a great company car. Plus I had a huge amount of freedom to work how I pleased. Essentially, my job was to follow cultural and economic trends so that I could help predict how those trends would affect thirteen-to nineteen-year-olds entering the workforce. I would then liaise with employers and government to make sure that young people were encouraged to move into industries and professions where there were job opportunities. I also watched for signs of market saturation so I could pass information back to the government, which would inform them if it were likely that there would be a reduction in new jobs in an industry or field.

Life was hectic. I had a young family and a full-time job that sometimes required me to drive up to 1500 kilometres a week. I was also involved in my local community running a youth group, and also owned my own music studio where I taught hip-hop and singing. Life was *definitely* hectic.

As I climbed into my company car – a white Holden V8 Statesman – Kate and the girls stayed at the door to wave me off to work. There was a little L-shaped dent on the roof of the Statesman just above the driver's seat and Milly always thought it looked like a love heart. We felt it was a good omen of love and protection as I set off to work each day.

I had a couple of meetings and a lunch appointment in Burnie, about 150 kilometres from our home in Launceston, which is where I have lived most of my life. It was a little after three in the afternoon when I said goodbye to my lunch companions, clearly remembering shaking their right hand, not knowing that this was the last right-handed handshake I would ever experience. I began the journey home and about ten minutes out of Devonport, a city half an hour away out from Burnie near Parramatta Creek, I was driving down the Bass Highway and fell asleep at the wheel.

In my semi-conscious state I drifted across the road into the oncoming traffic. The driver of the oncoming truck thought I was trying to commit suicide. I wasn't. I was just exhausted from trying to keep so many balls in the air and something had to give.

What gave was the side of my sedan. The first driver had successfully swerved out of the way, but the driver of the semi-trailer behind was not so lucky. Police estimated that on impact, the truck driver and I were both travelling at a combined speed of around 206 km per hour. The first impact spun me around several times and ripped open the entire right side panel of the car. Within a fraction of a second another car, which had been travelling behind the truck, ploughed straight into me – and I mean straight *into* me. Without the side panel there was no protection whatsoever. I can still hear the terrible impact of that final collision.

That was my kairos moment.

When Kate was told of the accident a friend rushed her to the hospital. Unfortunately there was only one way to get there and it meant driving past the scene of the accident. One of the worst moments of her life was recognising the little L-shaped love heart on the roof of the mangled Holden, and wondering how anyone could have escaped alive.

In truth I didn't escape alive initially. Six months after the accident I was in a wheelchair having dinner at a restaurant and I was approached by a guy who wanted to know if I was the man from the Parramatta Creek accident. It turned out that he was a coroner's taxi driver. He'd been informed that there had been a really bad accident on the Bass Highway and he was probably going to be needed to collect a body – mine! Thankfully the paramedics successfully resuscitated me when they arrived on the scene.

My right arm was destroyed, I broke six ribs, lacerated my liver, punctured my kidney and both my lungs collapsed. I dislocated my hip and my entire quad muscle was ripped from the bone on my right leg. My cruciate ligaments had torn and I shattered my femur, knee cap, fibula and ankle and lost the nail on my right big toe. I was devastated about losing my right toenail!

Yet, as far as I am concerned, I was incredibly lucky. First, no-one else was badly injured. Second, I was alive. My accident certainly changed my life, but as Greek philosopher Epictetus once said, 'It's not what happens to you, but how you react to it that matters.'

So often people talk about bouncing back after disaster, crisis, tough times or difficulty, but my body was broken. There was no way I could ever *bounce* back to the old Sam Cawthorn. It wasn't physically possible. I began to obsess about this idea and started to research resilience and how others had overcome incredible obstacles and pulled off amazing comebacks. In countless cases individuals and businesses used great challenges to forge ahead and create a better life or even greater success.

Nothing in life stays the same for long. Change and challenge are constant – although the curent speed and complexity of change means that we can expect upheaval every few years. World economies are still reeling from the Global Financial Crisis that began in 2007/08. Business is getting tougher and tougher and yet there are still success stories everywhere you look. Clearly some people have instinctively tapped into the power of bounce already and learnt how to use the inevitable difficulties of life as a springboard into something better.

No-one is immune to challenges in life. Bad stuff happens to everyone regardless of wealth, background or education. For some their crisis will be professional – losing a major client, having to adapt to a changing market during an economic downturn or being made redundant. For others, their crisis may be personal – the breakdown of a relationship, serious illness or, like me, physical injury.

Pain is inevitable, it is part of being alive, but misery is optional. I knew that I had two choices: I could give up, listen to the doctors who told me I'd never walk again and wallow in misery and bitterness. Or, I could accept that things had changed and use the crisis to reinvent myself and get better. I chose the latter. The challenges we face in life are not meant to be some sort of punishment, but rather they are an invitation to change – and an opportunity to create something even better than before.

Since my accident I have experienced excruciating pain, but I have also become stronger, happier and more determined because of it. I have come to understand the transformative power of acceptance and have developed a process to help businesses, organisations, teams and individuals go far beyond 'recovery' or 'bouncing back' to create revolutionary change by *bouncing forward* into greater joy and success.

Too often when crisis knocks on our door – whether professional or personal – we either ignore it or use all our energy and resources to try to go back to the way things were. We scramble to fix the problem so that it either goes away or life somehow goes back to the way it used to be.

I believe that the reason crisis sometimes destroys people or breaks their spirit is because they are fixated on what used to be. All their efforts are directed toward trying to recapture that experience or way of life. But sometimes there really is no going back. There is, however, *always* a way forward. I'm not promising that it's going to be easy, but if you find your road map through crisis, you can bounce forward into a better life.

My crisis demanded full recalibration. I lost my arm and I still have several physical limitations; I can't, for example, bend my right leg. But I honestly wouldn't change a thing. Everything that has happened in my life, including my accident, has made me the person I am today. In 2008, two years after my accident, my wife Kate and I welcomed our son, Jacob, into our family and I now live a life I couldn't even have dreamed of before my accident.

And if I can do it – so can you. Remember, pain is inevitable; misery is optional. Forget about trying to recover what used to be. Instead, embrace the crisis and use it to bounce forward into a life that is bigger, better and brighter than ever before.

The happiest people don't necessarily have the best of everything, but they make the most of everything.
                                                              – Sam Cawthorn

Sometimes things just don't go according to plan.

In January 2005 my younger brother David was diagnosed with acute lymphoblastic leukaemia. He'd not been feeling great for months and eventually went for tests and that's when they discovered the cancer. He was only nineteen years old.

Initially Dave had radiation treatment and chemotherapy. It was terrible watching him lose his hair and become weaker and weaker, but we all believed that he would beat it. Initially the treatment was successful and David went into remission. But in 2006 it came back and it was clear that his leukaemia was no longer responding to treatment. The only way he would survive is through a bone marrow transplant. Bone marrow is not like a blood transfusion – you have to find someone who is an exact match and it is a very painful procedure for the person donating the bone marrow.

I come from a family of eleven children; my mum is from India and my father from Scotland. I am number nine in the order, and my brother David number eleven. The best chance of finding a match was to test all the immediate family members, so the whole Cawthorn family were tested.

When the results came back there were only two matches – me

and my older brother Tim. At the time Tim was going through his own tough times so I volunteered to be the donor. I flew to the Bone Marrow Institute in Melbourne with David. By this point David was very sick and couldn't stand for long. I remember lying on the bed as they were taking the bone marrow, which was excruciatingly painful. David came up to me, crutch under one arm, the other arm holding on to his drip and he put his hand gently on my shoulder. We just looked at each other in silence. I knew how grateful he was that I was helping him and the pain eased away as we looked at each other.

A man who becomes conscious of the responsibility he bears toward a human being who affectionately waits for him, or to an unfinished work, will never be able to throw away his life. He knows the 'why' for his existence, and will be able to bear almost any 'how'.

– Viktor Frankl

The great news was that the bone marrow transplant was successful. David's leukaemia went into remission again and we are all over the moon. It felt like a weight had been lifted from the whole family and we could all start to look forward to the future. Then a few weeks later I had my accident. When Kate called my mum she was with David at the Bone Marrow Institute and the two of them caught a plane to Tasmania immediately. I can't imagine how hard that must have been for my parents. By this point they had been helping David to fight his cancer for over a year, and just when things started to look better for him, I was in a car accident. Mum didn't even recognise me when she saw me for the first time in the intensive care unit.

There were funny times too though – David and I comparing notes and arguing about which condition was the most life threatening. We'd always been competitive! We'd always been close but we became even closer through the bone marrow treatment and he would visit me often during my recovery. He was my best friend.

But our luck didn't hold. In June 2008 I broke my leg again and we were told that David's leukaemia had come back with a vengeance. He had about six weeks to live. Kate and I visited as much as we could, although by this time Kate was heavily pregnant with our third child and my own recovery had been put back by my slip on the ice. To add to our grief my dad, Peter, suffered a heart attack and was also in hospital. It was an extremely difficult time – losing David at the same time as we were getting ready to welcome a new member of the Cawthorn family seemed bittersweet for all of us. Emotions were running high.

Thankfully Dad made a full recovery, but David died on 16 July 2008. I can honestly say that losing him was far worse than losing my arm. Death is a strange thing – even when you are expecting it and you know it's coming, it's still a shock. We all believed that he was going to make it – even at the end. He'd successfully defied the six-week prediction and we took comfort in that. My parents took it especially hard – no parent should ever outlive his or her own children. I think they blamed themselves in some way, thought that perhaps their faith hadn't been strong enough. But no matter how much we wish or hope or pray, sometimes things don't always go according to plan.

We all know this, but somehow it's still a shock when it arrives. It's like we assume terrible things just happen to other people and that somehow our family or our business or our friends will be immune to the randomness and unfairness of life.

Things may not always go according to plan, but even in our most difficult times, we can be grateful. David taught me to be grateful. He reminded me just how precious and wonderful life can be – even the horrible bits. He may not be with us anymore but we enjoyed our 21 years together. We laughed and we fought, we fell out and made up and laughed some more. I would have preferred longer but sometimes things just don't go according to plan. We owe it to ourselves and the people left behind to be grateful for what we do have.

To this day I am sad that David is no longer with us, but his memory reminds me every day to celebrate what I do have. It's not just injury that can bring people down: stress, loneliness, failure, pressure and seclusion can do it. Thinking about how things have gone wrong in your life can be really disheartening, but you need to learn how to snap yourself out of it, count the blessings you do have and move forward. Be grateful and make the change.

It doesn't matter that I've lost my arm or my leg doesn't work. I know in my heart that I am blessed. I still have the most amazing wife and the most amazing kids who love me unconditionally. This is my reality check. None of us can afford to take life for granted. You are alive today for a reason and a purpose. I'm alive today for a reason and a purpose. I don't take a moment of that for granted anymore. I enjoy an amazing life, and I love what I do and I love having the opportunity to help others find their own way through crisis.

When you foster an attitude of gratitude you open yourself up to more positivity, which in turn fuels success. At the University of California, psychologist Sonja Lyubomirsky has studied the best ways to boost positivity and happiness, and gratitude is a real winner. Simply by taking the time to consciously count your blessings – even once every week – will increase your satisfaction and happiness levels. Psychologist Robert Emmons from the same university also found that gratitude improved physical health, raised energy levels, and relieved pain and fatigue, going so far as to say, 'The ones who benefit most tended to elaborate more and have a wider span of things they're grateful for.'

Happiness cannot be travelled to, owned, earned, worn or consumed. Happiness is the spiritual experience of living every minute with love, grace and gratitude.

— Denis Waitley

Thoughts and recommendations
Tim Sharp

Sam's story speaks for itself. It's inspiring, compelling, motivating and remarkable.

It's difficult to single out one lesson because Sam's whole story is a lesson. In fact, Sam's whole life is a lesson – in so many ways. Just reflect for a few moments on all the challenges Sam faced and all the hurdles he had to overcome ...

- An incredibly traumatic motor vehicle accident that he really shouldn't have survived.
- Multiple, serious injuries, which many people would struggle to cope with.
- Psychological trauma on top of physical trauma, which I know well from having treated many clients can be incredibly distressing and disabling.
- On top of all this, Sam had to find a way to financially support his family, emotionally reconnect with his wife and children, and find meaning and purpose to guide his post-accident life.

Not only did Sam survive all this, he thrived. He's thrived individually and personally, having created a highly successful public speaking profile and a growing speaker training business. He's also thriving socially by helping many others to find their voice, find their own ways to rise above difficulties and flourish in their own lives.

For someone like myself – who spends much of his time speaking and writing to express and communicate complex psychological and emotional phenomena – when I read or contemplate Sam's story I find it hard to say anything more than … wow! At the same time, having had the opportunity to get to know Sam a little during the writing and compiling of this book, I can say, with all due respect, that he's just another person. A remarkable person, sure. But just another person like you and me.

Having read the more complete version of Sam's story in his book, I'm confident that there's nothing he did – or does – in his life to survive and more recently to thrive, that you or I can't do.

And I'm pretty sure that's the message he'd like to communicate to you too because if it were only super-people who could achieve what he has, there'd be no point telling this story: it would only have meaning and lessons for other super-people.

I believe, and I know Sam concurs, that we can all practise the principles and apply the strategies that he used to make his life what it is today – one filled with happiness and success and gratitude and joy.

So how can you do this?

Following are the four principles Sam writes about in his book that he cites as being behind his ability to transform crisis into success:

1. Crisis creates opportunity

This sounds a little clichéd. I know that when I'm facing a crisis, opportunity isn't the first thing I think of. But every single successful person I've ever coached, met or heard speak has said something similar.

You see, happy and successful people haven't always had it easy. In fact, all of them, in some way have faced adversity and experienced setbacks. But they've all found a way to turn this around and create an opportunity out of the chaos. In some cases, it takes time. In all cases, it's not easy; but it's possible and if others have done it then so can you.

So whatever it is that you're facing now (or have faced in the past), ask yourself what you can learn from it. How might it make you stronger? What could you do to get through it and how great will it feel when you do?

2. Proximity is power

Positive psychology and social psychology research has, in recent years, accumulated more and more findings that conclusively prove we are, to a large extent, the product of the people with whom we spend the most time. Those you surround yourself with at least partially determine your success and happiness and health in life.

Sam and all the wonderful people in this book from whom I've learnt all surround themselves with positive and supportive people. They spend more time with those who lift them up and less time with those who are critical or undermining.

So if you had to pick your best possible team from today on, who'd be in the line-up? You don't have to completely abandon anyone who might have a tinge of negativity about them, but you might want to limit the time you spend with some and actively seek to spend more time with others!

3. Leverage positivity to fuel success

Several leading lights in the field of positive psychology have all come to the conclusion in recent years that in contrast to what many of us believe, and how many of us were raised, it's not so much that success leads to happiness but that happiness leads to success.

American happiness researcher and author Shawn Achor, for example, wrote about the 'happiness advantage'. And Professor of psychology Barbara Fredrickson has produced reams of research supporting her broaden-and-build theory of positive emotions in which she argues that positive emotions are extremely beneficial because when we experience them, we broaden (become more open minded and creative and therefore more resilient) and build (on our internal and external resources).

I have published a few papers on what I call the primacy of positivity, which I offer as the antidote to the tyranny of when. That is, rather than thinking you'll be happy when you achieve something or life's perfect or you have more money etcetera, if you can get happy now and create real and meaningful positivity right now you'll find yourself with more energy, inspiration and motivation to achieve what you want and need to achieve.

So find ways to boost your mood by having fun and using your strengths and connecting with others, and then use the positive energy that comes from this to fuel your success.

4. Bounce forward, not back

Set your goals high. Bouncing back after adversity might seem like a good goal, and it is ... but only if you're happy with good.

I think we should aim for great! Which is what Sam has done in his life.

Bouncing back might be a good start but what happens after that? Getting back to some sort of normality might be progress. But why stop there? As all the contributors to this book show, there's so much more we can all do – for ourselves and for others.

Michelangelo once said that the greatest risk to man is not that he aims too high and misses, but that he aims too low and hits!

Don't aim too low; don't settle for mediocrity or okayness.

Sure, take things one step at a time and allow yourself to recover and regain strength (physical and psychological, as needs be), but then go for gold! Use the stories in this book to inspire you to create an even better life in the future than the one you've had in the past.

A quest for life

Petrea King

If our health system were one that prioritised compassion and care, empathy and the engendering of hope, Petrea would be our Chief Medical Officer. She is the founder of the Quest for Life Foundation, which offers meditation, counselling and support for people living with cancer, grief, AIDS, depression, anxiety and other traumas. I've been lucky enough to know Petrea now for almost a decade. Every time I speak with her I feel better and want to be a better person. I hope in reading her story you too can enjoy some of her positive and inspiring energy.

It was in a tiny cave outside of Assisi that my whole life finally came unstuck.

At the time I was very unwell, having been told the leukaemia I had been diagnosed with the previous September would end my life by the Christmas that had not long passed. I was still alive but still unwell, still in turmoil.

This little cave, the Grotto of St Francis, became a refuge. I was desperate for peace and reconciliation with the past events of my life and the hopelessness of my future. The facade that I had meticulously maintained for most of my thirty-three years had irrevocably slipped to the floor of the grotto – and I with it. I became an inconsolable black hole of despair, remorse and self-loathing.

If it weren't for the love of strangers I would not have survived. An elderly priest, Father Ilarino, was the Superiore of the Eremo delle Carceri and he cooked, shopped and cared for me, a complete stranger. My life ground to a halt in that tiny grotto where St Francis used to meditate, pray and sleep. I loved the madness and the wildness of St Francis and shared his passion for nature and animals. I found nature wondrous and the behaviour of animals of all descriptions made far more sense to me than the confusing way people behaved. St Francis felt like good company for my distressed state.

I need to backtrack, though, in order to bring perspective to my situation as I saw it, in the grotto.

I was the youngest of three children with two older brothers, one eighteen months older than me. His name was Brenden and, growing up, he was a chaotic presence in our home. He exhibited ADHD twenty years before anyone knew what it was and he spent his childhood falling off the roof, breaking bones, decorating the house with lipstick, clinging to my mother or emptying porridge onto his head each morning. Being a little younger than he, I tried as hard as I could to be invisible, to have no needs. For me it became second nature just to 'split off and disappear' – and not have any needs.

Brenden told me before he was ten that he knew he had to

take his own life by the time he was 30. I immediately took that on as the reason for my existence. 'That's why I'm here. I'm here to keep Brenden safe.' I adored him, but I also found him really challenging, scary and difficult. He was incredibly bright, gifted with music, art and creativity and his large presence filled our days.

At the age of seven I had a profound spiritual experience that left me confused and added to my feelings of being different. I was running in the garden with my pet dog, Brynner, when suddenly the whole physical world became completely insubstantial. I was a part of this blinding beneficent Light that was far more real than the physical world. I could see through the earth, the house, my dog and the trees and none of it was solid. The only way I can describe it is to say it was like suddenly seeing the hand inside the glove; the glove being everything that was material but the hand being that which enlivened everything. While it was a very powerful, indeed profound, experience, I didn't discuss it with anyone as language to describe it was – and largely remains – beyond my reach.

When Brenden reached his teen years he went into major depression and was hospitalised on and off for years. He took awful drugs that turned him into a zombie and he underwent electric shock treatment. I found everything that was happening to him to be totally awful. I felt responsible that I wasn't able to help him even though I was only a young teenager myself. He attempted suicide several times before he finally succeeded in taking his life in Kathmandu when he was 32.

When I was eleven, I grew 23 centimetres in one year. My

knees swivelled in and started dislocating and I was unable to walk without constantly falling. After months of physio, I left school at thirteen and entered hospital where I spent the next three years having a dozen corrective surgeries and learning to walk again. The surgeon cut my legs at the femur and turned my lower legs outwards. Then he cut the tibias and turned my lower legs inwards as well as transplanting the tendons under my knees and shortening some muscles while lengthening others. After one of the surgeries I was in traction for nine months because the femur wouldn't unite and my doctor said that I would never walk again. After so many months in bed, my legs looked like two white hairy sticks attached to my body and, even with all my willpower, I could not move either of them.

However, when I was told I would never walk again, my steely determination kicked in. Every night between nurses' rounds, I would unhook myself from the traction unit, struggle to get out of bed and, taking my weight on my arms, manoeuvre myself around the bed. I could feel my bones grinding and this dislodged the plate and screws holding my femur together; however, the bone completely united in three weeks.

I returned to theatre to have the plate and screws removed as they were lodged in the muscles by my nightly activities. Of course, the doctor wondered how and why my bones had suddenly healed, albeit slightly crookedly, but I was too scared to say what I'd been doing at night for fear of criticism or punishment. I was also throwing most of my food out the window as I had a loathing for bedpans and had figured that if nothing went in, nothing would come out. This led to me being quite anorexic – my poor bones weren't receiving the necessary nutrients to heal.

Because of the unspoken spiritual experience I had at seven and then this hidden secretive life in hospital, I developed a split reality of being someone very privately to myself and the 'me' that I kept highly polished for everybody else. In our family no matter what was happening, we always coped and we never talked about how we felt; we only talked about what we thought. The attitude in our family was that we could (and would!) cope with everything. Perhaps this stemmed from never wanting to be a 'bother' because Brenden was being a much bigger bother!

As a child and young teenager I felt quite depressed and overwhelmed by the world. Why is it such a painful place? How come I have food while kids in Africa don't? How come I'm going to heaven because I heard about Jesus and yet those children will burn forever because they didn't hear of him? Why are humans so cruel to one another and to animals; so thoughtless about nature and the environment? I couldn't bear a God that allowed such suffering, so I sacked that God very early on when I had the experience of seeing beyond the material world. That had been such a profound experience for me. I *knew* I was more than my physical body and that there was this unacknowledged dimension to life.

During my hospitalisations I had several out-of-body experiences. I suffered with terrible cramps in the leg where the femur wouldn't unite. The cramp would start in the toes and move right up through the arch of my foot, my calf and leg, all the way into my hip. By then, I would usually pass out with the pain or I would find myself on the ceiling looking down at my body. From there I could see my body going through the motions of the cramp but the 'ouch' – the pain – went out of it. It was very confusing; I knew I wasn't my body because I was watching it going through the pain, but 'I' was alright and I felt fully alive, beyond the pain.

While in hospital I devoured all the books in their library, which was housed on a trolley wheeled around by volunteers. I would listen out for the familiar squeak of its wheels because new reading material was on its way! I read Krishnamurti, Alan Watts, the Bhagavad Gita, the Upanishads, Thomas Merton, Aldous Huxley and the Bible among many others including anything on animals, nature and astronomy. I devoured every encyclopaedia and studied the dictionary to learn words so I could catch my grandmother out at Scrabble, which we sometimes played for hours. Given that I never returned to school, my education and vocabulary came from these books and writings – and playing Scrabble! As a child and then teenager I was always curious about life. I was trying to find answers to all the great questions about existence. I taught myself to meditate when I was seventeen and it has remained a constant in my life ever since.

After recovering from the dozen operations and teaching myself to walk again, I went into nursing which, of course, was too physically demanding for me after so much reconstructive surgery to my legs. Within a year, I had damaged my spine and was confined to a back brace. It was during this time of again being laid low by my body that I was raped by a 'friend' at a church fellowship meeting. I was lying down resting in the bedroom of the house where we regularly met when this man overpowered me with his strength and desire. If I had called out for help it would have been provided, but I didn't have a voice. I was so used to being quiet, to not being a bother, not rocking the boat, disappearing somewhere else beyond the pain, beyond the humiliation and the fear. I felt, 'You can do what you like to me, I'm not here.' It was some years before I told anyone about that experience as I had felt it was my fault because I didn't call out for help. I didn't even think of it as rape because I was to blame.

At eighteen I ran (limped!) away to the country feeling defeated by life and relationships. I craved the stillness and solitude I found in nature as it made far more sense to me than people did! I worked in western Queensland outside of Cunnamulla and from there I went to New Zealand for a year, then Holland, then England for another couple of years, finally returning to Australia at the age of 24.

Because the arthritis in my legs impacted quite heavily on physical activities, I voraciously consumed information about diet and lifestyle and the positive impact they might have on my health. I'd become a vegetarian at seventeen and undertook a number of lengthy fasts of several weeks, sometimes just with water or freshly made juice. On my return to Australia I studied naturopathy, massage, homeopathy and herbal medicine. I wanted to understand the relationship between food, lifestyle, the mind, our attitudes and health as I intuitively knew that there was far more to healing than the medical approach that always seemed to be shutting the gate after the horse had bolted! No-one seemed interested in the context or story that people held about their illnesses and yet I knew that my story had a direct impact on my recovery from the many surgeries in hospital.

I knew the mind had a lot to do with health. I noticed how different my body felt when I meditated rather than when I felt overwhelmed by fear, anxiety, hopelessness, depression, self-loathing and despair. However, no amount of meditation helped me deal with these powerful and overwhelming emotions. I knew how to escape them by meditating, but meditation didn't resolve the underlying story that permeated my life.

Quite soon after returning to Australia I met Leo, who was soon to become my husband. We married and had two beautiful children, Kate and Simon. Unfortunately, though, in addition to his many wonderful qualities, my husband was also violent and the marriage lasted about eight years before its rather sudden ending.

After I completed my naturopathic studies, my husband, children and I moved to a community in America so we could do our yoga and meditation teacher training. We had been there just four weeks when I thought Leo had gone for a long walk, but he'd actually returned to Australia with all our money, leaving me stranded with two small children in a geodesic dome! Brenden had recently taken his life and I was already feeling overwhelmed by grief, loss and trauma.

Not long after Leo left I became very weak and ill. After two bone marrow biopsies and blood tests, I was diagnosed with acute myeloid leukaemia and was told that I would be dead by Christmas, just three months away. My very first reaction was relief. I felt in many ways that my life was a constant struggle. I was so weary of having to keep up appearances when really I felt helpless, hopeless, grief-stricken and tired of living with chronic pain.

It's a longer story, but finally I arrived in Assisi and stayed for several months in the Eremo delle Carceri, which was built around a series of caves that St Francis and his disciples used for prayer, sleep and meditation.

Each day I would spend up to eighteen hours a day in the Grotto of St Francis. It was there that I realised I'd used meditation for many years to avoid my feelings. I had many disciplines around mindfulness and concentration that kept my mind focused so as to avoid experiencing any of the complex feelings that lay just under the highly polished surface of my life. So finally, in the cave, it all came unstuck. I wept for weeks. I meditated, prayed and wept; meditated, prayed and wept.

Father Ilarino was an amazing presence in my life as he willingly took care of me. He had no English, I had no Italian, yet our conversations ran deep around life, love and matters of the heart and soul. I think, too, he was worried that he had this pale, skinny, divorced Anglican of Jewish descent holed up in his little Catholic cave. I think he thought I might die in there, but he was determined I wouldn't die in his precious grotto!

The first night he dragged me upstairs to sit at this ancient table where he put in front of me a meal with meat in it, a goblet of wine and a big chunk of white bread. As a naturopath I'd been saying for years, 'The whiter the bread the sooner you're dead.' I hadn't eaten meat or drunk alcohol, wine, tea, coffee or anything like that for fifteen years. So it was as if my whole belief system was there on the platter. I realised it was far more healing to be grateful for what he'd lovingly prepared for me – a stranger – than for me to say, 'I can't have what you've lovingly prepared because my belief system says no.'

It was profoundly humbling to realise that I knew zip about anything. For all my studies, qualifications, my understanding and knowledge, I knew nothing about love, about trust, about letting go. It was the first thorough dismantling of my beliefs. I knew how to live my life if I clung to those things, but what I couldn't do was trust in life. 'I'll do it myself' was the dominating belief that underpinned my life. So instead of that I started to practise seeing that I was in the palm of life/love/God, and there was nothing I could do that would ever separate me from the realisation of that except what was going on in my own mind.

There were times when I was in a morass of self-pity. I felt totally unworthy and unlovable, and I became completely self-absorbed. I was my own universe and couldn't see past it as I obsessed about not being good enough, of being a failure, a loathsome person. And yet, I could see so clearly that focusing on those thoughts would perpetuate my suffering. I felt trapped in my own miserable mind and, while it was not an easy path,

I could see that there was nothing more worthwhile than to liberate myself from this kind of sick thinking. This meant liberating myself from self-hatred and judgement because, if I was going to die, I wanted to find peace before doing so. As these beliefs fell away, gradually peace became my more constant companion. Time passed and the more I dismantled my beliefs and wept tears over trying so hard to get it right, to measure up to some impossibly high self-imposed standard of perfection, to save Brenden – and the world! – I felt stronger and more at peace in the moment.

When I came back after several months in the grotto, I desperately wanted to be with my children. I wanted the peace that I had come to, to remain. I wanted that peace in my relationships; I wanted that peace to remain with me in all aspects of my life. I knew that peace was not dependent on being in my body. My *preference* was to live but I wasn't *addicted* to having to stay alive, because I knew peace was not dependent on remaining in my body.

So I returned to Australia, saw my doctor and had the first blood tests for many months. He told me I had zillions of baby red blood cells and that I was in an unexpected remission from leukaemia. He assured me that leukaemia would return as soon as in a few days or weeks. (I suspect one reason I may have developed leukaemia was that I had dozens of X-rays as a teenager. Portable X-ray machines were new and I had one every other day to see if the bones in my legs were uniting – and I was never appropriately covered to protect my body from radiation.)

I found living with uncertainty very challenging. When you know you're going to die there are things you need to say and do, and I'd done and said all of them. I had my will and financial affairs in order. I'd made tapes and letters for my children for the future. I'd given my children to the care of their father. I had my whole life all packed up ready for the big trip … and then the plane got cancelled and I went into remission. How much do you unpack the suitcase? How much do you live as if you're really going to be here? It took some months, but then I realised that everyone is living with uncertainty, they just don't know it. Those of us who have had many traumas in life know that life can change in a phone call, a moment, a breath or a conversation – and it's never the same again.

I lived in this place of great uncertainty until my mother said, 'Have you thought of working?' This came as such a surprise! I was living in the transit lounge of life forever waiting until my flight was called. I rang Marcus Blackmore from Blackmores Ltd and he told me, 'Forget what your doctor said. There's a doctor in Sydney looking for a naturopath to go into practice with him. I'll introduce you.'

So I went into practice as a naturopath and, within the first two weeks, the first woman with breast cancer came in. The day after, the first person with AIDS came to see me. Both of them had been told that they wouldn't see Christmas, which is what I'd been told fifteen months previously. I felt they were fellow travellers in the transit lounge of their lives and I knew what a challenging and difficult place that was for me.

My question to people has always been, 'What is it that stands in the way of you being at peace?' Sometimes it was nausea, insomnia, pain or night sweats and I'd adjust their diet and/or use herbs and homeopathics, meditation, mindfulness or other therapies to alleviate their symptoms. It's hard to have peace of mind if you don't have peace in your body!

'Now what is it that stands in the way of you being at peace?' Our conversations led into deeper issues as they would say, 'I don't know who I am. I don't know why I'm here. I don't know what my purpose is. My mind is out of control. My relationships are in tatters. I hate myself. I'm afraid. I want peace. I need forgiveness.' These were familiar issues for me and these amazing and inspiring people helped me understand, and in time articulate, the inner human journey we are all on – the journey to peace and wholeness.

The conversations with clients went ever deeper into the arenas of meaning, of purpose, of forgiveness and wholehearted acceptance. The more I was just present – without judgment, creating a space for the unutterable to be spoken and witnessed – the more my clients seemed to feel understood and helped. I provided a safe space in which people could utter the anguish or give expression to whatever caused them distress. Who am I? What am I doing on the planet? Am I living the life I came here to live? If not, why not? And what am I going to do about it? Those were the questions I had grappled with and they had been a driving force in my life.

Even now, thirty-one years later, I find it a great privilege to sit in a circle of people with extraordinary stories. Stories about illness, trauma, disaster or diagnosis, we call them the Ds: drama, disappointment, disability, death, divorce, disloyalties, disfigurements, disagreements, depression – there are lots of Ds! And when you bump into these Ds in life, everything that's second nature no longer works.

It might be second nature to drown our sorrows, to drug ourselves, to fill ourselves up with so much busyness that we don't have time to feel. It might be second nature to blame other people for our misery, to resent other people's happiness. It might be second nature to us to isolate or fall into an habitual pattern of, 'I'll do it myself.' But this D, whatever it is, causes us to realise that whatever has become second nature to us no longer works. You'll often hear people say, 'It's second nature for me to feel like this/react like this/think this way.' It is interesting that we often talk about what is second nature to us without ever wondering about our first nature, our essential nature, before we took on the fears, anxieties, limitations and habitual beliefs that impel our behaviours.

It seems to me that the purpose of human existence is to relinquish everything that has become second nature to us so that we reveal, experience and live, in our first nature, our essential nature, which is home to love, compassion, wisdom, insight and the source of our creativity. We sacrifice all of those wonderful qualities the moment we project into the future our fears, worries and anxieties or we're consumed by resenting, blaming or the shaming of our history. It's a letting-go of all mental constructs or beliefs born of our wounds. Once we've let go of the construction there's just the moment, the stillness and our place in it. The less we construct the better because then we experience the moment with freshness and without judgement.

After a while, I worked from home because I started support and meditation groups and we had over 200 people in our sunroom each week. I worked for a couple of years with prisoners with HIV/AIDS in Long Bay jail and at the Albion Street AIDS Centre conducting support and meditation groups for eleven years.

In the very first cancer support group I ran there was a woman with breast cancer named Kay and her partner Wendie. I didn't know Wendie so well, but Kay came to support groups for several years. In this time she grappled with the highs and lows of her illness and finally her impending death and the leaving of her three beautiful children and her beloved partner. Before Kay died she told Wendie, 'When you're over the worst of the grief, go and see what you can do to fluff Petrea up because who looks after her?' So Wendie became a volunteer and, before long, my partner of now 23 years. We are very fortunate to have each other and not a day goes by that we don't acknowledge with amazement and gratitude the life and work we share together.

In 1995 Wendie and I moved to Bundanoon. A couple of years later Killarney House, a 35-bed guesthouse in 9 picturesque acres, came on the market for $1.5 million.

The Quest for Life Foundation that I established in 1989 had only $15,000 in its account. We were missing some commas and zeroes! I had always dreamed of providing a safe place, just as I had experienced in the Grotto of St Francis, so that other people who were distressed by the events of their lives could find solace as well as learn practical skills to meet their challenges. One of my clients gave me a slip of paper with someone's name on it and said, 'If you're serious about purchasing this place then ring these people.' These wonderful people, who have always chosen to remain anonymous, enabled Quest to purchase and refurbish the buildings so that they were suitable for our use. We opened in 1999 and have been busy ever since, providing retreats for people living with life's great challenges of cancer and other chronic illnesses/pain, grief, loss, trauma, PTSD, depression, anxiety, the consequences of bullying or past physical, sexual or psychological abuse and so on.

Now, people travel from all over Australia and beyond to the Quest for Life Centre in Bundanoon to find a safe place in which to utter what has been unutterable and, once heard and deeply understood, they can learn practical skills for managing their life and its challenges. It puts them back into the driver's seat and allows them to find a profound sense of meaning about the events that have been a part of their lives.

The aim of each program or retreat is to help people actively contribute to their health and wellbeing and establish peace of mind. It's about living today well. The capacity of the human spirit to embrace great suffering is just extraordinary and is very inspiring to witness. We recognise that we can't always change what happens to us in life, but we can always change how we respond to the challenges that come our way. Otherwise our suffering gnaws away at us until we deal with it, or it embitters us, or it kills us. We can feel as angry, miserable or depressed as we need to, for as long as we need to, because what happened to us may well be a terrible thing. But we all recognise that staying stuck in that place of anger, depression or misery isn't going to help us find peace.

I well remember the day in the grotto when I realised that there was nothing and no-one to blame for my misery. I could still be sitting there now – a dusty little pile of bones in the corner of the cave – muttering, 'It's not fair!'

It wasn't fair that I grew up with Brenden, not fair that he told me he had to kill himself, not fair that I'd spent years in hospital dealing with considerable pain, not fair that I was raped, that Brenden attempted suicide so many times before he succeeded, not fair that I married into violence, not fair that I was crippled with arthritis, not fair that I was diagnosed with leukaemia, but that didn't change the fact that all those things had happened to me.

I needed to weep the tears and reconcile with my past in order to find peace in the present and build resilience for the future; not the armoured kind of resilience that I had so long relied on but a soft, open ability to be present to the moment regardless of what it contains. When the mind is quiet we have access to our intuition, wisdom, creativity, insight, humour and more. These are powerful allies when dealing with the uncertainties that profound change can precipitate in our lives.

In our programs and retreats tears are welcome, but there's always a lot more laughter than tears. There's a great power of possibility in a group of people who all understand suffering, even though their suffering may be born of different causes.

We have very experienced teams of six that work on our retreats comprising two facilitators, two support people, a trained counsellor and a massage therapist. In addition to their professional qualifications our retreat team members and teachers have considerable life experience that has included suffering. You don't arrive at a place called peace and unpack! Peace is a moment-by-moment choice.

Given that this work has provided us with the opportunity to work with more than 100,000 people living with considerable challenges, I believe we have developed a profoundly beneficial program that allows people to reclaim their peace of mind and make meaning of their circumstances. We talk about the journey of being human, which is based on neuroscience, epigenetics and an understanding of a holistic perspective. We discuss sleep, nutrition, the role of exercise, switching off the mind, living mindfully, forgiveness, making meaning of suffering, managing our time, communication strategies and a host of practical skills that equip people to deal more effectively with their challenges. It is a continuing source of joy to meet people whose lives have been transformed since they attended a support or meditation group, had some counselling or attended a workshop or retreat with Quest.

People often arrive at our retreats feeling disheartened or desperate for peace. Just as Father Ilarino took care of me, a stranger, all those years ago, we endeavour to love people back into wellness. This often means bearing witness to their anguish, rage, grief, fear or despair before they are ready to embrace concepts about peace or healing and how to attain them. What matters is that people feel profoundly heard and that someone gets them. I've also learnt through long experience that people have their own best answers and, if we provide a safe, non-judgemental environment in which they can begin or continue that journey, people can discover their own best approach to the situation or challenge they are facing.

When you nearly die, and then you don't, you're faced with the question, what now? What's a good way to spend a life? How do we reconcile our suffering and make meaning of the traumas and tragedies? I am grateful for the journey that my life has travelled as it has made of me a better companion to people embarked upon their own suffering. Being with people who understand the inner landscape of powerful emotions is profoundly helpful. If we all shed a little light on one another's paths, we will all find our way home to peace and wholeness.

Thoughts and recommendations
Tim Sharp

I first met Petrea about a decade ago when we were both invited to be part of an amazing panel discussion organised by the Smith Family. There were a number of inspirational and impressive speakers and I was honoured to be part of a great event.

Although it was relatively early in my public speaking career, I had already been lucky enough to share the stage and program with some fabulous people. But not everyone appears or behaves the same when in, and out of, the spotlight!

It was obvious that Petrea King was the real deal. Her presentation, a mini-version of what you've read in this chapter, was outstanding and fascinating. But her manner – with me and with every member of the audience with whom she interacted afterwards – was what struck me. All these years later, I've never forgotten how she behaved: with genuine and authentic care and compassion, love and interest, for all. I was incredibly impressed by her humility and modesty, her lack of grandiosity or self-congratulatory language.

Every time I meet with Petrea, and luckily for me this is a semi-regular occurrence as we often cross paths at functions, events and conferences, I'm reminded of her true passion for life and her true care for all with whom she comes into contact.

How does she have such an effect?

It's because she genuinely cares about life and health and happiness for all of us!

Before I met Petrea, I did some research about her and her background as I did with the other speakers. I like to be prepared, and part of that is knowing my fellow panel members and conference speakers as well as I can. I knew a little about her story and I'd heard some of what had happened to her, but I was awestruck by Petrea's story and by her amazing resilience and recovery.

But just as much so, I was unforgettably struck by one relatively minor fact about her and her story: the name Petrea chose to call her organisation.

Now remember, Petrea was close to death, and then decided to help others who were close to death (or diagnosed with a life-threatening illness). This is pretty heavy stuff! So what did she decide to call her work?

Quest for Life!

I loved it; and I loved it for all sorts of reasons. At the time I was waving the positive psychology flag largely on my own here in Australia, but I was passionate about focusing on positives and working towards thriving and flourishing, not just surviving. Quest for Life seemed to embody this approach completely and beautifully.

Essentially what she was telling people is that if you come and work with me, regardless of how many days you have to live, we'll help you live them to the fullest! And this is what I take most from Petrea's story, and her life, and her wonderfully warm way of interacting with me and anyone else who's lucky enough to enter her world.

Life is for living! Even if you're not 100 per cent healthy; even if you've faced or are facing trauma; even if your health or your relationships or your job or anything has gone bad. You can still make the most of what you have, with what you've got, from where you are.

- Prioritise health and wellness – regardless of how healthy you are now. I'm not suggesting, and I know Petrea never claims, that diet or meditation or herbs or supplements will save your life or cure terrible illnesses. But as part of a sensible approach to life and living, they can certainly improve *quality* of life. (We know for a fact this is true for exercise, meditation and healthy eating.)

- Forgive and love – holding on to hurt and bitterness achieves nothing of value to anyone involved. Forgiving and letting go is often easier said than done, but it's undoubtedly worth the effort. And loving, unconditionally, as often and as well as you can is also one of the best things we can do for our own health and wellbeing, longevity and quality of life.
- Help others – this is one of the most effective ways to help ourselves. In service we gain so much; by giving we receive. I can completely relate to Petrea's mission to help others as I know how much I gain from my work. I know Petrea gains as much from what she does for others as they gain from her.

Emotionally fighting fit

Cynthia Morton

Cynthia has worked in the field of emotional fitness since 1995 as a speaker, author and workshop presenter. Cynthia believes wholeheartedly that language has the power to sabotage or save our lives, and that the skill or negligence with which we articulate our emotions through words either builds or destroys the quality of our public and private relationships. Her work has earned her a multitude of national awards, including The Pride of Australia Medal, The Prime Minister's Award of Excellence, an Australian of the Year Award (local hero category Qld) and Award of Distinction for Services to Humanity (from the Australian Medical Association of Queensland). Cynthia is the author of A Helping Hand With Life *and* Emotional Fitness.

My anger has meant pain to me, but it has also meant survival.
Before I give it up, I'm going to be sure that there is something at
least as powerful to replace it on the road to clarity.
— Audre Hordes

I have been asked quite a few times over the years by clients, colleagues and people in the media what my take is on childhood tragedies. Horrific stories are being reported more and more on the evening news revealing childhood violence and sexual abuse scandals. So often these upsetting crimes are perpetrated by trusted public figures. In my case, it was at the hands of trusted private figures.

Having grown up as a little girl amidst two sexually violent predators that threatened to kill me if I ever told anyone, I've done many years in therapy shaking with rage, calling them every obscene name under the sun I could think of.

Like many of us, I have needed to grieve the loss of innocence in my childhood as well as parental death and marital death. Refusing to do the work in my youth, denying my grief, created the birth of full-blown addictions. There is always a price to pay for emotional self-negligence.

Our grief won't just go away.

We cannot bury it long-term; we've got to grow up and face it or it will bury us in a lifetime of fear and misery. It's not true that we just need to give our grief time. Sure, time is an element in building emotional fitness, like it is when we choose to build our physical fitness, but time alone does diddlysquat.

We have to emotionally show up and face any grief, trauma and pain in our past. Regardless of whether we are grieving a lifestyle (for me booze and drugs were a complete lifestyle and my loyal emotional lovers), a country, our innocence when we were kids, a career, or even our children leaving our nest. Death and feelings of emotional abandonment through betrayal, natural rites of passage or emotional negligence are all deep blows of loss to our hearts.

I now understand that grieving any loss is important because it allows us to free-up the emotional energy still clinging to the lost person, place or experience. Once we have processed our heart's pain we can then reinvest that loving energy elsewhere. Until we become willing to work out our pain we will find emotionally reinvesting difficult; a part of us remains tied to the past.

Once we have learnt how to endure, process and recover from deep grief, we become emotionally fitter. When we have loved and lost, grieved and healed, we are gifted with a deeper gratitude and a braver heart. Healthy grieving is an active process that we all need help with. If we ignore the self-care required to grieve, the price we pay is remaining immobilised and emotionally frozen, feeling numb and on pause.

Grieving is not forgetting. Nor is it drowning in tears. Healthy grieving results in our ability to remember the importance of our lost love or lifestyle with a newfound sense of peace rather than immobilising pain.

Many survivors of trauma blame themselves because our perpetrators taught us that it was our fault. We of course believe them. When a traumatic event occurs, we go into shock (denial) involuntarily as an automatic protective device. As we reel in pain, denial temporarily buffers us from the full impact of a direct blow straight to our poor ol' heart.

Our capacity for denial enables many of us to survive; following our bliss with an open and trusting heart has never been taught and just seems overwhelmingly dangerous.

Those of us still clinging to our beloved denial, however, are not being cowardly or deceitful; we are simply trying to survive with the only emotional tools we have. We need help, not ridicule, to gradually learn to really comprehend how our denial works.

When you ask a goldfish in a bowl, 'How's the water?' the little goldfish is likely to respond with, 'What water?'

Denial becomes a dark way of life we often don't realise we're in: we're too immersed in our familiar behaviour (like an innocent goldfish) to sometimes even see it. Yes, it may seem we are lying to ourselves and others, but we are often naive to our own lack of self-awareness.

I love the acronym that explains this often misunderstood and harshly judged word D.E.N.I.A.L.

D for DIDN'T
E for EVEN,
N for KNOW
I for IT'S
A for A
L for LIE.

If we make a decision to start to heal in adult life, we get the best bang for our buck if we become willing to surrender our weapons of mass distraction. I am referring to booze, drugs, food, sex, spending, gambling, workaholism and so on.

Then we learn how to sit with the emotional heavyweights: anger and sadness. It would be unhealthy to not be angered at horrific crimes such as childhood abuse. Anger is a natural stage of the grieving process we are often told; yet this knowledge holds little comfort.

Anger for those who have never experienced anything like a traumatic dehumanising act is healthy and natural. To hear about it on the news will invoke humanitarian anger in most emotionally connected, concerned adults. However, rage is often experienced for those like me, who have faced varying degrees of physical and sexual violence first hand. Rage is also a natural occurrence for any parent, sibling or spouse to experience when finding out the incomprehensible event of sexual or physical abuse has occurred and that someone they love has been violated.

When I hear all the name calling, rage and anger directed at perpetrators ousted in the media from some in our community, I empathise and understand only too well how they feel. However, there are some among us who have processed their anger and rage then fallen in a heap of despair and depression, feeling like they will drown in their sadness. That is also a natural and healthy response as we process our grief and gradually heal our hearts.

I have cried oceans for the innocent little girl I once was, aged four.

I would often lie underneath the lemon tree after two sexual assaults in one evening. This usually happened on my birthday as excessive alcohol was consumed on this date as other elders had birthday celebrations that were also held on the same day. As a result I was often babysat by the paedophile next door on my birthday.

My small bruised and throbbing body climbed into its avatar pod under my favourite lemon tree the day after my birthday.

In that sacred space my daydreams transported me to another land where fairies rode on sparrows' backs wearing glittering butterfly gowns. So, at four years of age, I learnt that birthdays, Christmases and any biological tribal event where excessive alcohol was consumed would always be the worst days of the year for me.

My elders would often put on a birthday party for me in the paedophile's garage next door because it was big and under shelter. No need to go into details, but let us just summarise: as the day progressed I would be pulled consistently onto his lap and chastised for not smiling and being an ungrateful child.

My elders would then go out to celebrate with a birthday dinner. This meant leaving me to be babysat next door with more unspeakable situations arising for my little body as I was left in his care. Being carried and put back into my bed by a second predator at the close of the evening left me feeling a suicidal child long before I even started kindergarten.

At this time in my life two male predators had been committing horrific crimes against my femininity for quite a few years already. It continued for another four years. Groomed to put on a smile and be a good girl or boy is what too many children learn how to do and this is why it's still so prevalent. It goes undetected to an untrained eye for sometimes a whole lifetime.

I have been working on my own emotional fitness healing wounds from my past since 1995. I had to finally face my alcoholism and drug addiction that had spanned nineteen years. When I surrendered my addictions, I was a single mother of two sons living on a pension. Removing my beloved emotional anaesthetics like booze, drugs, three packets of cigarettes a day plus handfuls of pills left me in a foetal mess on the floor. The tsunami of sewage from my childhood abuse rendered me mute and hospitalised with chronic post-traumatic stress disorder. So I started to write and my first book, *A Helping Hand with Life*, was born. Putting pen to paper to give my heart permission to finally speak saved my sanity and my life. I share the same drive for writing as Robert Frost: 'I write to find out what I didn't know I knew.'

So when Dr Timothy Sharp and I met by chance as co-presenters at a conference in Sydney in 2003, consequent discussions resulted in us deciding to co-author my second book titled *Emotional Fitness*. It is still a steady seller today, so when Tim invited me to contribute to his new book, I was absolutely delighted to be able to return the favour.

The birthing of my two books had a domino effect, leading to my desire to create The Emotional Fitness Foundation in 2004. Helping others in my present instead of blaming and shaming those in my past has been transformative and healed my once untrusting fearful heart. My past traumas took me to a very dark place of suicidal despair where too many of us remain for our entire lives.

My work with Emotional Fitness helping indigenous communities, abused children, teens and mums and dads has received almost unbelievable honours such as the Pride of Australian Medal, Prime Minister's Award of Excellence, Australian of The Year Award (Local Hero category in

Queensland) and the Australian Medical Association's Award of Distinction for Services to Humanity (Queensland Branch).

Over the past twenty years I have worked in jails and drug and alcohol rehabs; however, these days it is mostly in mainstream society.

A pivotal point for me was working face to face with sex offenders and learning more about this tragic human issue (without rage and fear dominating my heart) with genuine interest. I needed to understand what was going on with these two men I loved dearly, yet feared, throughout my childhood.

I knew my healing was robust when a young, well-dressed corporate client dropped into our inner city Emotional Fitness Centre in Brisbane a few years back. He was perhaps 25 years old. He worked for a big law firm, was incredibly handsome, well dressed and obviously highly intelligent from the way he articulated himself in our daily Emotional Fitness groups. He had attended EF groups for a few months, so he knew my story as I led the groups and shared often.

One day he asked for a private session. In this session he started by stating, 'If I tell you this, Cynthia, I'll understand if you never want me to come back or ever lay your eyes on me again.' He was shaking and could not make eye contact.

'I've never admitted this to anyone, ever, and perhaps shouldn't now.' He put his head in his hands and sobbed.

I asked if I could touch him; he didn't respond, just curled into a deeper foetal ball and silently wept, he seemed inconsolable. I rubbed his back as I would if one of my sons was upset.

'Just cry it out. I'll help if I can, and if it's any consolation there are not many toxic and tragic stories I haven't heard before,' I said, doing my utmost to reassure him that I would not add to his pain.

More silence, more sobbing. At least 30 minutes passed.

I lit a scented candle and just held the space for him. He eventually started to speak very quietly but clearly.

'I haven't acted on anything, I promise you. I promise you I've never had sex with anyone; I'm too terrified of my sexual urges. I'm still a virgin.' I remained silent and he continued.

'Cynthia, I hang around playgrounds. I think terrible sexual thoughts involving children. I'm so scared of myself. Please don't hate me, please don't hate me, please ...'

All I could see was his courage to be asking for help. I felt no desire to call this tormented soul names or shame him in any way.

'I'm going to help you. We will make an appointment here and now for you to speak to a specialist who can and will help you. Do you trust me? Can I make this call, now?' He nodded.

I had been doing a great deal of voluntary work with a variety of charities as an ambassador, so I'd been working with some of Australia's leading specialists in this area. I phoned a skilled therapist I had been working with. I explained the situation and we made an appointment for him later that day.

He went. He was immediately hospitalised.

You may not agree with my approach and I absolutely defend your right to disagree with me. I do, however, know through my own experiences and through being exposed to amazing leading experts like Dr Timothy Sharp, Professor John Saunders, Dr Frieda Briggs and Dr Beres Wenck, teachers and ambassadors of love and compassion, that those of us who have barely survived life can absolutely heal and use our past as a platform for triumph and learn how to thrive in life.

This was just of the many beautiful and constructive pivotal moments I have been gifted to experience in my emotional recovery. I spent so many years wading through deep grief, feeling hopeless, useless and incompetent in life, so moments like this when I have felt hopeful, useful and helpful are priceless.

I sincerely hope my sharing this event might be helpful in some way at some time. Little Cynthia is now safe; she is a whole and healed part of me now. I dedicated my first book to her and in the closing pages of my first book, wrote a poem to that child lying underneath the lemon tree.

Little Cynthia used to imagine that the sparrows visited her under that lemon tree when she was deeply traumatised. She imagined these friendly sparrows carried fairies on their backs that only she knew were there. Invisible to the eye, these divine pretty little fairies had a magical way of removing the horror with enchantment and breathtaking beauty. I would like to share the poem my adult self wrote to my fragile, brave little child self with you.

The Mighty Sparrows

My heroes, my lifesavers, my beautiful friends
So small but so mighty
Silent to the end.
No words needed, just gentle comfort and a smile
Always come to visit, but only stay a little while.
Cannot hold you, cannot touch you
My heart knows you must be free.
A busy bird; many souls need you
Not only me.
With your blinking eyes and twitching head
A vision that brought me peace.
Without your friendliness and time
My belief in beauty and freedom would surely cease.
A small, soaring soul, magnificent in its plainness
No one to impress, many just pass you by.
A wise and gentle messenger
You helped me believe my soul would one day fly.
Can't do this book without you
Am I worthy of this flight?
Please stay with me dear sparrow
Help me believe, in the deep, dark quiet of the night.
We have come so far together
Don't know how much more to go.
I see you at the bread shop
I look for you everywhere I go.
Thank you my darling sparrows
My life's heroes, you always make me smile.

Cheeky fat little tummies
You have made all the pain worthwhile.

I did not cut and paste that poem just now. I chose to retype it out. Each line massaged my heart as I remembered typing it back in the year 2000 for the very first time.

Now as a woman in my mid-fifties I have remarried and am as happy as a clam. My sons have grown into two beautiful, impressive gentlemen. I am still one-day-at-a-time clean and sober, and I feel fit. Emotionally fighting fit.

So what did I find to replace all my denial, anger and sadness? Awareness, compassion and kindness. Putting love before ego takes real emotional muscle in adult life, but we do not have to do it overnight – just one moment, one hour, and one day at a time. Consistent baby steps are the magical key.

So was all the therapy, the pain, the confronting emotional work all worth it?

Absolutely!

Our wounded heart, if we honour its grief, can and will heal, and living can become a truly beautiful, safe and abundant experience. Really.

Thoughts and recommendations
Tim Sharp

When I first met Cynthia I felt like I'd been hit over the head with a piece of two by four! I rwas shocked by the detail she shared in her story but at the same time, I felt a deep sense of admiration for her brutal honesty and remarkable courage.

As I've read and re-read the various contributions to this book, the concept of honesty seems to reappear. Honesty with oneself as a first step to change; honesty with others as a necessity to building truly meaningful relationships; honesty with and about the world more generally in order to really live and thrive.

And there's no doubt that Cynthia honestly faces up to life's cold, hard realities; there's no doubt she pulls no punches – when dealing with her own issues and when helping others deal with theirs.

At the same time, however, Cynthia beautifully balances brutal honesty with empathy and compassion; she's inherently a caring and considerate and loving person and this comes through in every interaction I've had with her.

The combination and integration of these traits is also at the heart of what's enabled Cynthia to overcome grief, forgive (herself and others) and so effectively move on. Consider what she's experienced, what's been done to her and how she's suffered; consider also where she is now, how she currently lives and what she's done in recent years to share her knowledge and experiences to help others.

So what did I learn from Cynthia's story? What do I think are the most important lessons to be learnt?

In short, and at the risk of oversimplifying, anything is possible; and the overcoming of anything is possible.

Of course, it's not easy, but what I feel when I read Cynthia's story and what I hope you will feel is something akin to hope; something like optimism. I hope you'll enjoy thoughts along the lines of, 'If she can do it then maybe I can'; 'If she's overcome and moved on then surely I can.'

But how? Some of the tips I'd recommend based on Cythia's story are:

- Begin where you are and do what you can with whatever you have.
- Change what you can change, accept what you can't and be wise enough to know the difference.
- Learn from the past but don't dwell in it.
- Look to the future and be prepared to work hard to create a better life.
- What Cynthia came to label emotional fitness is a great metaphor because just like physical fitness, emotional fitness takes hard work and diligence and consistent effort.
- Work out what exercises (eg meditation, thought challenging acceptance, goal setting, communication skills training etc.) you need to do and develop a program that involves doing them every single day.
- Finally, Cynthia has gained much from helping others to gain; by helping others she's helping herself. So find ways you can help others and through selfless acts you might find you selfishly improve your own life!

Rising out of depression

Lana Penrose

I was lucky enough to be asked to review one of Lana's books recently, The Happiness Quest, *and I was very impressed with her combination of honesty and humour. As you'll see when you read her story she's been through some incredibly difficult times, but her perseverance and courage and the comedic twist she seems to be able to put on even the most distressing of events is admirable and so very likeable. What I found and what I hope you'll find as you get to know Lana is that learning to laugh in the face of challenge is a valuable and enjoyable lesson to learn.*

I guess the best way to acquaint you with my story is to draw you straight into my black hole of despondence. Several years ago, I was a woman in her thirties known for her literary prowess and dubious sense of irony. I had a bestselling book under my belt, came from a loving family and was living the dream in an apartment overlooking a spectacular vista of crashing waves, emerald green grass and rugged coastline. Yet despite having it all, my mind often churned out thoughts like these:

I'm dripping with self-hatred. I've just spent over an hour crouched in the corner with my head in my hands. Infinite sadness wells from the depths of my soul. I literally cannot stop crying.

I've told myself over and over to get over it. I'm a grown-up, for goodness' sake. I need to get a grip. Only I can't. I'm in the throes of another debilitating episode and it feels like being devoured. So I cry and I cry as I rehash all that's wrong with my life, which is, well, everything. I fantasise about death. It's a sick place to go, but I can't seem to help it.

My life seems continuously muddied by these feelings of defeat, loneliness and a macabre sense of worthlessness. I feel like a fraud – a useless shadow of a human being. Inside me is a void. I know I need to save myself but every day feels more excruciating than the last and I don't know if I can keep fighting.

I pray for these deadly emotions to go away and never come back, only they always return and it's always the same. No matter where I go or what I do, this thing seems to stalk me; forever lurking in the shadows, watching, waiting: a predator poised for attack.

Sometimes things subside and I'm convinced the chase is finally over and I will never be hunted again. But then, there it is, snarling in my face. I see the look in its eyes and know that I'm about to bear the brunt of its violence.

I can't stand this for much longer – the non-stop abuse that loops inside my own head. Nobody understands what this is like and I feel so alone. This is overwhelming. I'm close to giving up. I want to fall asleep and never wake up. This condition will kill me. But suck it up, Lana, because this is your life.

Have I inspired you yet? Yeah, thought so!

In case you hadn't gathered, I'm a former sufferer of clinical depression, although at the time, I didn't quite know what the heck was going on. I only knew that it felt like my life was out of control and pretty much sucked. And that was because whenever this thing had me up against the wall, it was as though it had never left me and never would. The height of its onslaught would last for a day or two before receding slightly, but it was always there, hovering, hiding, sniggering behind pot plants with seditious intent. Although I sensed that it couldn't wait to sink its teeth into my throat again, I'd go about my business but usually, within a week, I'd find myself devoured by despondence yet again. My life sort of became like watching *Apocalypse Now* on repeat ad infinitum. It was thoroughly exhausting.

As time slowly passed, I spent ages trying to figure out why I felt the way I did. Why couldn't I cast these horrendous feelings aside? Was it self-sabotage? Fear? My lot in life? Life itself? Perhaps I was genetically disadvantaged, or an emotional sponge absorbing the earth's negative ions. Or maybe it was the vast chasm between my soul's purity and the chaotic world outside my front door. Maybe I wasn't properly plugged into The Source. Maybe I'd listened to too much gloomy music by The Cure during my misspent youth. Maybe it was this. Maybe it was that. The rumination was ceaseless.

The only thing I was certain of was that nobody would ever get the way I felt, and no amount of wanting to feel another way made any difference. I so wanted to embrace life and be like a happy-go-lucky person in a four-wheel-drive commercial who whacked on a seatbelt and grinned until her face all but fell off rather than being perpetually locked in a brace position. I so wanted to be like a frivolous sitcom character – social, fun lovin', fancy-free and living it large. It's just that … I wasn't.

Instead, my chest literally ached. Fear and regret tumbled through me always. I berated myself for aging, for failing, for my stupidity and worthlessness. My past sickened me. The world frightened me. I felt frustrated. People weren't treating me as I ought to be treated. Hang on. Yes, they were. They were treating me like rubbish because, quite simply, I was.

How in God's name had I become like this? I mean, I wasn't always this way. It must have had something to do with moving countries a few times, trading Australia for Greece, then Greece for the United Kingdom before returning home with my tail between my legs. Of course, my divorce hadn't helped. A montage often flashed through my mind: Husband. Smiles. Athens. Frowns. Separation. Tears. London. Confusion. Alcohol. Air guitar. Misery. In the closing scenes of this tableau, I was not only a woman exhibiting low self-esteem, I was a low self-esteem engine. I then went on to accidentally date a drug addict – a guy who, unbeknownst to me, was secretly hoovering heroin as I innocently swept the floor.

Generally speaking, my thirties did my head in and there's only so much a person can take. After returning to Australia after seven years of crazy, I therefore strapped on a pair of rollerblades and teetered on the precipice of sanity. The last unfortunate episode had jumped on top of the one before that, which clambered on top of the one before that – a pyramid of woes swaying like a knife-wielding acrobatic troupe balanced on a unicycle, complete with goofy clown horns, raspberries and an explosion of silly string. That's when the bad memories and negative self-talk began in earnest and created neural pathways in my brain that became so well worn that I could offer a guided hiking tour through my head.

In essence, I felt trapped, immobilised, pathetic, embarrassed, ashamed, self-loathing, isolated and steadfast in not wanting to burden others with my woes. I didn't get why I was unable to take Taylor Swift's advice and simply shake it off. For the most part I kept things to myself and as a result, every day became just that little bit harder, and the depths of my sadness became like a dirty, dark secret – like privately rearing an eight-limbed baby with a hairy back, too gruesome for the world to see. I felt suicidal.

However, there's another side to this story. Each of my tribulations led me to really stop, think and take the bull by the horns. I mean, seriously, what the hell was this thing and what could be done about it? Despite being consumed by melancholia, I knew that I had a choice, and I decided to use all the strength I had to get up, dust myself off and grin like a village idiot. When overwhelming emotions next rocked up brandishing knuckle-dusters, I vowed to at last stare them down, despite feeling like a pathetic, legless kitten mewing from a box. And honestly speaking, I thought I had about as much chance of rediscovering happiness as converting a slice of cheese into a colony of aardvarks.

My first port of call was to a general practitioner who asked me to complete a questionnaire. For the first time in my life, I was officially diagnosed with major depression. I know it sounds obvious now, but at the time I was gobsmacked. I knew I had depressive symptoms, sure, but major depression? I mean, come on! How depressing! And couldn't they have come up with a less daunting label, like Major Inconvenience, or Major Tom as a salute to David Bowie? In any event, upon receiving the news, my condition suddenly felt hot, razor-sharp, frightening and very real.

In a funny way, though, it opened up a new opportunity. I now had something more tangible to work with and that's when I decided to really dig deep. There was a fork in the road and I was going to rip it out and stab at life's steak. The time was right to throw all that I had at dumb-old depression. My quest for happiness therefore began.

I entered cognitive behaviour therapy.

I leapt around like a gazelle to boost my serotonin and dopamine levels.

I entered schema therapy.

I chatted with a close associate of the Dalai Lama.

I entered EMDR therapy.

I extended forgiveness.

I read a mountain of books.

I underwent acupuncture.

I attended spiritual workshops.

I practised gratitude.

I exercised philanthropy.

I extended compassion.

I practised mindfulness.

I watched *What the [Bleep] Do We Know?*

I drifted through alpha, theta and delta states while listening to raindrops, gongs and flutes as though holidaying in Phuket with Jethro Tull perched on my bedhead.

I meditated my neck off.

And after a great deal of time and soul searching ... nothing happened.

Absolutely nothing!

I remained as depressed as ever.

But after a solid block of time that involved facing the darkness, feeling uncomfortable, crying my heart out, dredging my psyche, getting up and falling down like Chumbawamba personified, I finally reached a point where I broke on through to the other side. Yes! I really did! And looking back, I saw that each and every one of the above endeavours to overcome depression and re-experience happiness airlifted me that little bit further from the treacherous waves of Lake Quagmire. But before I get too ahead of myself, allow me to take you back to one of the early parts of my healing journey.

Meditation was a major contributor when it came to realigning myself with me. Even though I'd tried it over the years, it had actually been closer to me sitting for extended periods of time and sifting through every conceivable thing that was wrong with my life. I'd also think about things like how chewing a cooked chicken wing must be identical to tucking into a human finger; how weird it is that our species is like a sprawling herd of animals pretending not to be a sprawling herd of animals; how weird it is that sound projects from a hole in our faces; how gross it is that a roasted leg of lamb is a roasted leg of lamb; and how horseracing is, in fact, animals riding animals while other animals watch on from the sidelines, cheering and wearing hats. I naturally concluded that I'd never really nailed the art of meditation.

So in the early phases of my happiness quest, I attended a Buddhist workshop to lay the foundations for inner peace. A Buddhist nun offered this pearl of wisdom, which really struck a chord: 'We say we need someone or something to make us happy. But if things are agitated internally, we're unhappy regardless. We hope other people will change. We try to alter our lives. We can try to change the world, but it won't work. We'd be smarter to *change our minds*.' She was so right. And that's exactly what I intended to do. Meditation was the first stepping stone to achieving this and under her tender guidance, I, the novice, attempted meditation as my mind did its thing.

Breathe. Breathe. [Insert rude thought here.] Exterminate! Exterminate! Burst the distraction! Burst the bubble. Baths. Bubble baths. STOP! Breathe. Breathe. It won't be long now. Kylie. Bums. Spinning around. Back to the breath. Back to the bath. Back to the bums. Back to the breath ...

But relaxxx! I stuck with it, and after practising and practising, I eventually got the hang of it to the point of experiencing sublime clarity and serenity like never before. It just took gentle perseverance, and I can't tell you what a difference it made. Try it. You'll like it!

I also dabbled with medication. Under a doctor's supervision, I nervously popped a 75 mg SNRI capsule labelled with a brand name best suited to a science fiction character made of an indestructible alloy, and wondered how long it would be before I mutated into a futuristic motorbike. 'I've never experienced anything like this before,' I confided to a friend over the phone at the time as camels roamed my desert-dry mouth. 'It feels like my brain's been replaced by two cups of self-raising flour and a wet rag.' I then lolled about, dazed and confused.

Although medication often works a treat for others and its benefits are indisputable, sadly it didn't quite work for me. In the spirit of Goldilocks, I tried different dosages and types but my biology and brain protested dreadfully, and the rogue walrus inside my head continued tusking my cranium. Yes, my mind had a mind of its own, my ups and downs remained as pronounced as the menacing teeth of a cartoon shark's jaw. But did I stop trying? No way, man. Thankfully the avenues to equilibrium are many and varied.

I kept up my talk therapy, devotedly attending CBT and schema therapy week after week. Gradually I became more enlightened when it came to understanding the mechanics of my mind and why it was sometimes inclined to wobble. I ate well, avoided alcohol, exercised, fake laughed, socialised (a bit), visualised and skolled a naturopathic remedy that tasted a lot like rancid vase water. I also sprinkled a little EFT, NLP, kinesiology, distance healing and shamanism into the mix. Yes, I tried all these things, so determined was I to overcome depression. And I knew it wouldn't long before I'd be skipping about as though perennially lost in a breakfast cereal commercial. And yet I still wasn't.

So I engaged another element in my dynamic approach – something known as EMDR therapy, which stands for eye movement desensitisation reprocessing (is it any wonder they acronymised it?). This therapy specifically targets trauma that may lie behind some depressive conditions. And I have to say that this next little bit's a lot more difficult to write about than the rest, but it did help me to unravel something ugly from my past that remained stubbornly wedged within my psyche, so I feel it's important to share.

Although I seldom thought much about it, my first boyfriend at seventeen was psychologically and physically abusive. In other words, my introduction to love came rolled in a fist.

My EMDR sessions took me back in time with a view to relinquishing the pain associated with this confronting sliver of life. During therapy, I saw myself pinned to a wall, my face blotchy and swollen. I then saw my body in a heap on the floor. I listened to a young man threatening my life. Sharp, icy words. Cold, dead stares. Blows. Bruises. Threats. Empty apologies.

The day I left this guy had incited his deadliest rage. He'd dragged me into his car as I'd walked to a train station. He'd driven me past my place of employment and kept on driving. Filled with terror, I'd begged him to tell me where he was taking me and he told me in no uncertain terms that he was driving me to deserted bush land for the express purpose of murdering me. His dead eyes told me that he absolutely meant what he said, and there's no doubt in my mind that he intended to carry out his threat. I've never been more petrified in my life.

I screamed out of the car window to city pedestrians for help and found myself on the receiving end of shrugs and averted eyes. I spotted a police car, waved it down, and it vanished. Minutes later, a squadron materialised with sirens blaring. As the aggressor and I were separated – the glow of red sirens flashing across our respective pale faces – I didn't dare press charges, too terrified to see this man again, especially in a court of law, and especially when I suspected that he'd see to it that I'd suffer the consequences. On the advice of a friend, I did, however, visit a magistrate to take out a restraining order.

To a girl in her late teens, the magistrate appeared to have more accusation in her eyes than sympathy, and the steely way in which she spoke suggested that she believed I'd brought the circumstances on myself. Even to this day, I can't quite believe how I was treated back then, not just by the perpetrator, but by someone who was allegedly assigned to protect a victim of crime.

This part of my life was something that I'd mostly kept to myself, aside from sharing with a few friends, therapists and my ex-husband. Nobody ever seemed to really understand what I'd been through, least of all me, and the burning question always remained: how in God's name had a middle-class, well-educated and dearly loved girl who'd never been abused before in her life wind up in this situation?

Today I know that millions of women suffer similarly and that the young and the innocent are often easy prey. These girls can find themselves in such predicaments owing to their own sweet naivety and because they instinctively want to help the psychologically damaged abuser, as fruitless as it may seem. That was me.

Anyway, after I arrived home after the EMDR session that addressed this prickly issue and saw me reliving a nightmare, I began to wonder if the pursuit of happiness was really worth it if it meant dredging up my bleakest past. But after a few more months of processing other traumatic events in my life and meditating, and never giving up, something began to shift. My world view began to bend and change. I couldn't quite believe what was happening!

So after over two long years of doing all I could to conquer my demons and depression, I was stunned to discover that therapy actually *worked*, as did the majority of other things I tried in their own special way. The key seemed to be in tackling things from all angles, determination and unwavering persistence.

Towards the end of my quest, I distinctly recall taking a reflective stroll along the coastline one late afternoon as the sea put on a spectacular display below. In the fading light, intense teal waves, half a kilometre in length, crashed on the rocks and sprayed crystal beads high into the air, creating an unforgettable symphony before my eyes and ears.

As I watched waves collapse on the shore and pull back to regenerate, I gained greater insight into my life. I saw that I had entered this world to 'know thyself' and free my soul of unnecessary pain. I was not here to carry that pain around for the rest of my life and parade it around like a weeping battle wound.

My job was to learn all I could from all that had befallen me and pass that knowledge on before shedding this mortal coil. My job was to be the best person I could and contribute any positive energy I had to the collective consciousness. My job was to love.

As sea spray misted the air, I reflected on the pressure placed on people who didn't feel right to get over it and get on with it, when it seemed much wiser to allow them the opportunity to purge their offending feelings by doing whatever it took to set themselves free. For me, well, I felt exorcised and exhilarated because I'd been crazy enough (and lucky) to do just that.

I strode down to the sand, thinking about my day-to-day life. I usually wrote while overlooking a sparkling, ever-changing ocean. My body still worked, so I could swim, walk, even march in the KISS Army if the opportunity ever arose. I could schedule in meditation and visualise. I knew gorgeous, interesting people who'd suffered much rougher rides – physical afflictions, impossible upbringings, torturous circumstances, heavy abuse, disease, death and grief. To my mind, they were the true warriors, but the challenge for all of us seemed to be to overcome adversity as best we could, break free of any difficult cycles where possible and celebrate whatever victories arose.

And now that my mind was clearer, I saw that my life was flipping awesome! It had been all along, only I'd been wearing blinders and carrying around too much pain. A dirty black dog had often eclipsed the sun and rag-dolled me half to death, but now that I'd manoeuvred myself into a better position, I felt like I could punch it in the snout and laugh at its clumsy retreat.

Stupid depression!

Today, post-mindlift, I am delighted to announce that I continue to be happy, liberated and depression-free. No more agoraphobic weeping fests. No more self-flagellation. I cancelled my membership with the Mortician Appreciation Society.

In December 2010 – at the close of my happiness quest – I experienced one final vitriolic outpouring of pain and angst, then everything subsided, like the reluctant retreat of a storm. My depressive feelings never came back. I repeat. Never. The intense, overwhelming emotions I once accepted as a normal part of my day-to-day existence are no longer a part of me, which isn't bad going considering I battled erratic feelings to various degrees for many, many years.

I no longer entertain suicidal thoughts. I repeat. *Never.* Instead I continue to experience self-love and inner peace to a degree I never could have imagined possible and in such a sustained way. I feel unbelievably *free.*

Yup, my pursuit of happiness absolutely changed my life and the relatively short time it took to eradicate a lifetime's worth of baggage was absolutely worth it. My only regret is that I didn't do everything in my power to get to this point sooner. It would have saved me a truckload of bother.

The best part of all, though, is that I feel that everything I've been through, the whole kit and caboodle, has put me in a stronger position to be able to extend myself to others today. I now regard being of service as the main reason we're here and philanthropy has become one of my life's mainstays.

Post baptism of fire, I received my counselling diploma and I remain poised to help in any way I can, ready to lend a sympathetic ear and my depth of understanding to those who need it most. One of my favourite things to do is volunteer weekly for Lifeline as a telephone crisis supporter. For me, the gift of being invited into other people's lives during their darkest hours to offer comfort is the greatest privilege I've known. To describe it as rewarding isn't quite right. Rather, it is humbling, and I almost feel selfish in admitting that my Lifeline work serves to maintain my happiness, my offer of assistance perpetuating my sense of wellbeing.

It's kind of odd that through being a more connected, compassionate and contributing individual, I am able to maintain equilibrium and mine even greater joy. We've all heard stuff like this before – to give is to receive – but I've proved it for myself. And being able to negotiate life with this expanded outlook has changed absolutely everything – how steady I feel, how comfortable I feel within my own skin, how I perceive life, others and my own happiness levels overall.

It is my hope to maintain these feelings and continue working with those who suffer in any way I can. And to think that major depression got me to where I am now, well, it's almost inconceivable.

Today I continue to move unrestricted through life and for that I am deeply grateful.

Contentment is mine.

It is my wish that it is yours, too.

Thoughts and recommendations
Tim Sharp

I first read about Lana's story when her publishers, the publishers of one of my earlier books and, as it so happens, the publishers of this very book, asked me to review her latest effort and provide (if appropriate) a testimonial. I was more than happy to provide a testimonial because I can honestly say I loved reading Lana's book (*The Happiness Quest*).

I'm often asked to read self-help and self-development books, especially those that touch on happiness, and the reality is that their quality varies enormously. So I'm more than happy to support those I believe to be good, and/or those grounded in empirically supported methods, but there are some to which I simply have to say, 'Thanks, but sorry.'

Lana's definitely fell into the former camp and the reason I enjoyed it so much (as I hope you've enjoyed this chapter here) is because it was, in all my experience, quite unique. I'd read first-person accounts before, but never had I come across a personal story that so accurately described the experience of depression and anxiety – and did so with such incredible humour.

As I read Lana's *The Happiness Quest* I found myself vacillating between laughter and tears; between joy and sorrow; between fascination and fear.

And this is, for me, the greatest lesson we can learn from Lana and her amazing story. Not only does she beautifully describe her trials and tribulations, her successes and her failures, but she does so with remarkable comedic class so that her experiences, which to be honest are quite terrifying at times, become more palatable and ultimately more easy to consume and take lessons from.

This humour is at the heart of Lana's resilience; and her resilience is incredibly impressive. But many of us are afraid to use humour and playfulness during tough times; too many of us are afraid to laugh in the face of adversity.

I fully accept that there are times when it's hard to laugh and smile or make jokes; in fact, some situations should not be made fun of.

But that's different to not using humour because you think it's not respectful; or because you think people won't take you seriously; or because you think it will take away from the severity of all that you're facing. Humour, when used appropriately, will do none of these things – it can't.

But what it might do is help you through; what it might do is make a challenging situation that much easier to cope with; what it might do is provide you with the impetus to see the situation differently. Seeing adversity differently is one of the most important aspects of getting through tough times.

As Henry Ward Beecher once said, 'A person without a sense of humour is like a wagon without springs. It's jolted by every pebble on the road.'

Lana Penrose shows us all, among many other things, that humour can provide some shock absorption!

- Don't be afraid to laugh in the face of fear and adversity – it won't always be possible but where and when it is, it could

provide vitally important energy and perspective ... do
everything to encourage yourself to laugh.

• Keep trying – the first treatment you try or the first therapist
you see may not be the right or best one for you. I
recommend that you stick to treatments that at least have
some scientific support, and remember that many
treatments require perseverance and time. In recent years I
have come to the conclusion that different things work
for different people, and they'll probably work in different
ways for different reasons. So keep trying until you find
what works for you.

• Believe that happiness is possible! As Lana shows, we don't
just have to aim for an absence of depression or a lessening
of anxious symptoms (although that's not a bad start).
We can aim much higher. And although for some, life will
prove challenging on an ongoing basis for all sorts of
reasons, for many of us this need not exclude the very real
experience of joy and success and living a great life.

Rising above tragedy

Ingrid Poulson

Ingrid Poulson has inspired many through her own compelling journey of resilience. In 2003 her 72-year-old father, her four-year-old daughter and twenty-month-old son were all murdered by her estranged husband, who then killed himself. Since then, Ingrid has been working to change the way the police force deals with domestic violence, which has led to a change in police training and practice. She is now an author and speaker and advocate of RISE living, which incorporates the four values that are the cornerstones of her life: Resilience, Integrity, Simplicity and Enjoyment.

The single most important decision you will ever make is whether or not to believe in a good universe.

— Albert Einstein

I was standing in a coffee queue in a mall one day when a woman approached me. She was clearly agitated, her voice raised and her hands flapping, drawing the attention of everyone in the queue. 'Ingrid!' she started (although I barely knew her, she felt that she knew me because she had seen my face splashed about the media). 'How can we help you? What can we do? We've thought about a memorial. Maybe a garden? Is that what you want for them? What can be done?' She babbled on, not pausing to consider the effect of her words on the curious bystanders, not even taking in my own startled non-responsiveness. Finally, she paused, then looked me up and down before saying, 'Well, *you're* doing okay.'

Her tone was one of such reproach that I immediately felt awash with guilt. Her comment, though cutting, reflected exactly how I felt about it myself. I couldn't understand how I was doing okay either. It didn't seem right, didn't match the enormity of what I'd been through just a couple of months before. Why wasn't I curled up in a ball, or drunk, or not here at all?

To understand the woman's behaviour and my own, I need to take you back ten years earlier when I was 21 and dealing with the sudden death by suicide of my 24-year-old brother, Adrian.

His death scorched through our family, all of us clinging together but ultimately, having to work through the journey of grief alone. It shook my confidence in life, spinning me into dangerous behaviours, being careless with my body, mind and life. It was my way of showing my scars; letting the world know how much I loved and missed my big brother.

At the time of his death, I was just nearing the end of my first university degree. I managed to complete it and even spent a few months working casually, but his death was always around me. All my friends knew. I wore his clothes and smoked his brand of cigarette and felt exhausted and emaciated by my lack of nutrition and body care. Eventually, I decided to take the backpacking holiday to Europe that I'd been saving and planning for. In many ways, it wasn't unusual for someone of my age to go for a trip before settling in to the reality of a career, but the trip was really my way of fleeing the grief, to be among strangers where I didn't have to be that girl whose brother died.

My trip of five months ran closer to five years, involved many adventures and expanded from Europe to Asia, ending in Thailand where I lived for three years. Toward the end of that period, I met Neung, who became my husband and I returned to Australia expecting our first child. Our gorgeous daughter, Marilyn (Malee), was born in May 1999 and in October 2001 our baby son, Sebastian (Bas), joined the family.

Although we shared many happy moments, my husband and I soon realised that we had some serious differences on issues around child rearing and money management and our relationship became more and more fractured.

A few months after Bas' birth, our arguments became more heated, and Neung's behaviour toward me started to become threatening and then violent. The night after I barricaded myself in the room with the kids while he hurled items and abuse, I packed our things and left, asking my father (whose property we shared) to ask him to leave. Neung took the separation badly and after months of threats and increasingly aggressive behaviour, I went to the police and had an AVO placed against him.

He broke that AVO in the early morning hours of 15 September 2003, breaking into the house, binding and raping me at knifepoint.

Over that long night, I managed to persuade him that he needed to go back to work in the morning and, once he'd left, I called the rape crisis service and the police.

I asked my father to mind the two children (now four and nearly two years old), only telling him that Neung had breached the AVO and left with the police to go to the hospital. When Neung learnt that I had gone to the police, he went back to the flat and stabbed to death our two children and my father, who was trying to protect them.

At the time, the police were driving me home to be with the kids. When we arrived, Neung had attempted suicide but was still alive. I knew instantly that the kids and dad were gone, but I tried to wrestle the knife off him anyway. I still couldn't say for sure how I was then moved away from him, but I was sitting on the grass when they shot him and he died on the way to the hospital.

When they drove me away from that house in the police car, as I lay on the police station floor in the foetal position and then in the ambulance, I was beset by one simple question: 'Why am I still here?'

It was a question that stayed with me as I went to the hospital, as my family arrived and my mother took me back to her house where she and my sister and other family took care of me. A recurring question in the days and weeks that followed as I grappled with the loss of not only my children and dad, but my job, my home, everything I owned and my identity as a mum. The press that haunted our doorstep labelled me 'The woman who lost everything', the only headline that resonated with me as true. I was numb, shocked, bewildered, exhausted, twisted by nightmares, anxious, feeble, unable to make the simplest of decisions and yet, despite all this, despite even my reluctance to be a part of it, still going.

To be seemingly casually standing in a coffee queue in the mall a couple of months later, then, did seem jarring to both the woman and me. I couldn't give her an answer to her questions, both asked and unasked, and it was my wellness, rather than any sickness, that led me to seek out a medical opinion a few days later. The GP listened sympathetically as I faltered through my story and when I finished, she didn't reach for the prescription pad but instead explained that I didn't have to be depressed or suicidal. 'I am continually surprised,' she said, 'by the resilience of the ordinary human being.' Just like that, she had given me a word to describe what I was: not weird but resilient.

There were a number of turning points in my survival, and the naming of this word, resilience, was one of them. I started to see myself not as doing it all wrong, but as doing it my way, almost experimenting with my own survival story.

I didn't want to be remembered, recognised or defined as 'That woman who …' I was constantly referred to as a victim, and in particular, a victim of domestic violence, a label I abhorred. I knew that I had been the victim of an horrendous crime, but the label felt like I had just let it happen, hadn't rallied and fought and done everything I could to protect my family. It sounded helpless and passive. I realised that victim was more than just a state of circumstance; it was a state of mind.

What's more, I instinctively felt that there was a lot of permissiveness around staying in the victim role, and there seemed to be an amount of confusion and negative judgement around being, well, normal. Although I understood it, I didn't want to succumb to this social pressure. It was important to me that I didn't become a drunk or fearful of all men or consumed by bitterness and then blame my way of life on what had happened. I felt that my family deserved more than that; that I owed it to my dad and to my children to do something and be someone, to be above this act of vengeance.

I started to push down the judgement of people like the woman in the mall and even the voice in my own head about how I *should* be and started instead to explore how I *was*. It was some months later at the close of the inquest that my mother helped to summarise what my family and I were doing.

Referring to my sister, my father's wife, herself, and me, she stepped forward to address the gathered media and said, 'There's been a lot of talk about victims. We are not victims. We are four strong women. We are survivors.'

Her words kindled the hope within me that I, in fact all of us, were on the right path, not the path for victims but the path for survivors.

I wasn't quite sure in the beginning where exactly I was going or what I would do, but I did know, to some extent, what *not* to do. I'd learnt that from going through the death of my brother. Some months after the murders, I participated in a session where I described my experiences and the way I was managing my grief to a group of counsellors. Following my narrative, one of the counsellors remarked that my brother Adrian's death was like the grit that gets into the oyster shell; just as the oyster works and works at the source of irritation to create a pearl, I had worked and worked through the pain of my brother's death to create hard-earned pearls of wisdom.

I knew my brother's death had taught me about grieving, but I baulked at calling what I'd learnt pearls. Pearls are things of beauty, perfect and pure whereas the majority of my learnings felt half-formed to me, still grating, still needing work, still, essentially, in the grit stage. My grits of grief included:

- Grief was really confronting, physically and emotionally exhausting, a difficult, confusing and arduous slog.
- Traumatic death made the people around me behave unpredictably, and say and do odd things. I'd lost friends that I thought I would be able to lean on in hard times.
- No matter how much I ducked or dodged it, how much I travelled or lost myself in other ways, this death was a part of my life that I could not get away from.
- There was no pausing or concession for what I was going through – whether I wanted it to or not, the world in all its ferocity and idiocy, continued on.
- No matter how many times I asked, 'Why?', how much energy I expended, how much I worried about it, agonised and agitated, I could never, ever, really understand it.'
- It was really, really difficult to have to receive help from everyone else.

• There was no point in feeling good as any feelings of happiness or joy were always swamped by feelings of guilt.
• No matter what I did, how I behaved, or how badly I treated myself, it didn't *work*. Nothing I did changed what had happened. Nothing brought him back.

And now I'd learnt a final bitter truth – going through grief was not a warranty against going through it again. There was no immunity to tragedy and sadness. There could always be more.

I could hardly look at such a list with feelings of joy and optimism, with the thought that they were beautiful pearls. But it was true that I had learnt some very difficult things through my brother's death and the way I grieved for him.

Indeed, whether consciously or not, it was this knowledge that ultimately guided me to change the way I grieved. Many of the things I did were the complete opposite of the way I had handled my brother's death, because I knew that what I'd done ultimately hadn't worked.

Most importantly, and pivotal to the fact that I was in a mall and not curled up in the dark, drunk, was that I knew my family wasn't going to come back, *no matter what I did*. I knew that my body could not sustain enough damage, that the scars could never be big enough to demonstrate to the world how much I loved and missed my family. I knew that trying to take it out on myself physically, emotionally and mentally would never change the past. I realised, having been through it already, that I had no control over what had already happened.

The only thing I could control, I realised, was my response; my reality now. I knew that I couldn't get away from the grief, that I couldn't just stop it or escape it through travel or drinking. There was only one way through it, and that was *through* it. And if I was going to be in this life, go through this grief, and somehow honour the lives of my father and children, I simply had to take care of myself.

I was weak and emotionally wrung but generally physically healthy. I started to engage with this, reluctantly at first but then with more energy. I wrote a very basic list of what I wanted to achieve in a day and placed it on the wall opposite my bed. At the end of the day, I could mentally check things off. I headed it with 'I show I care for myself', which at that time was a very bold statement. It was very easy in those first stages to be completely undone by guilt and feel that I was to blame for what happened, that I had earned my misfortune and that I was not worthy of being well. The title, even on the days I didn't believe it, was a small reminder that I did, in fact, have value.

I show I care for myself by:

- Eating three pieces of fruit a day
- Eating five vegetables a day
- Exercising every day
- Drinking 2 litres of water a day
- Having at least two wine-free nights a week
- Keeping a high standard of grooming
- Setting goals
- Recognising my wins.

The list is almost embarrassingly simple, but it works. Even now, if I feel myself scraping along, I go back to the list (or one very like it) to sort myself out. It relied on the basics, mostly physical; something that I could control when my thoughts and emotions seemed wildly erratic.

My list was my way of choosing a response to a situation in which I had been rendered helpless.

Despite my determination to continue on, those first few weeks and months were mostly about keeping my head above water. Trauma left me feeling raw, vulnerable and exposed. I felt that I didn't have the emotional capacity to deal with all the pain I was holding onto, let alone what was going on in the rest of the world. What's more, the future seemed to be a massively overwhelming, impenetrable blank, leaving me flailing around for what I was meant to be doing with it. 'What am I going to do?' I asked myself over and over. When I finally asked the question externally, it was (thank goodness) to my mum who asked, 'Which bit are you worrying about?'

'All of it. The whole future.'

'You don't need to worry about that now,' she responded sagely. 'You just need to get through today.'

The day-by-day approach worked miracles. Sometimes, when even a day seemed too long, I took it down to moment by moment.

This approach started a chain of living small, what I called shrinking my universe. I started to whittle things down to a size that I could handle, small moments, fewer people, less input from the outside world.

A big part of that was limiting media input. Even living in a very sheltered environment, I had access to the news and newspapers and the headlines would catch my attention. Each sad story of loss or conflict affected me deeply until one day, I decided it all had to go. I let go of my built-in belief that in order to be a good citizen of the world, I had to be intimately involved with every painful detail.

I stopped reading the papers, turned away from stories on the internet and, after sending an apology out to the world, I got rid of my television. I know many people who no longer watch commercial TV, but at that time it was a fairly radical choice and a bit of a surprise to some. (It made my heart soften when some well-meaning friends, believing that my situation was financially motivated, offered to buy me a set.) I haven't gone back to the news since, and I can pretty much guarantee that nothing out there has changed. But my inner peace has. Earlier this year, I took a similar step by cancelling my Facebook account after realising that instead of being about my friends' news, it was rapidly becoming a conduit for world news (and lots of advertising around wrinkles/cellulite/weight loss). It's enough to make one paranoid!

In my new world of smaller living, I started to become very aware of my physical environment. I was drawn to natural or beautiful environments, needing to be among nature, colours or to find something attractive in my immediate environment that I could rest my gaze on. Ugly environments, litter, nasty graffiti, polluted drains, even crowds of unsmiling faces deeply repelled me. In the first days of my grief, the lights felt too bright and I listened to calming (mostly classical) music to soothe myself, relying on candlelight and drawn curtains to get through the day. Slowly, though, these started to feel quite repressive and I started to seek out more light, more colour, more upbeat music.

Even when I eventually moved out from my mother's house and set up a flat in a less-than-salubrious block, I made it as attractive as possible, adding plants, fairy lights and a cheerful swing seat outside, and using bright stripey colours wherever I could inside. I also maximised the amount of light I could get by rarely shutting the blinds and spending a huge amount of time outside. I was still having nightmares and anxiety, so I tended to sleep with the light on anyway. I am now lucky enough to live near a beach and staring out at the water serves as a balm to even the most tricky of emotional states.

One of the grits that I'd learnt from Adrian's death was that friends, even very close ones, can behave unpredictably, say awkward things or choose this time to reveal some horribly painful secret of their own or worse, just disappear. So, in a way, I was prepared for this, realising that I just had to let go of those who went and decide some time down the track whether we could be friends again.

Instead, I focused on the amazing people who arrived. Some were old friends made new again and some were new people who appeared in my life. Sure, some of these dropped off when they realised I didn't need rescuing, but there were some true gems who I treasure to this day. They weren't necessarily the ones who had the polished words or appropriate social refinements (if these even exist in traumatic cases), but they were there to listen and cry with and laugh with (yes, laugh with – we will get to that a bit later) and help me muddle through.

The wider community, too, came out in force, sending messages of love and support, lending us clothes and bedding, sending flowers, raising money, organising meals and helping to keep the media at bay. All this kindness helped retain my faith in the good of the world. I allowed it to nurture and coddle me, comfortable in the knowledge that I had gleaned from Adrian's death that there would come a time when I could pay forward all this love and support.

There were, however, other people who were not such a positive presence who were constantly down or seemed to be judgemental about how I was keeping up. I had no desire to join a misery circle and lament my lot. Instead, I felt it was important to protect the spark of life inside of me that yearned for a better reality. If I was around difficult people, I engaged emotionally with them as little as possible, nodding and smiling blandly and saying things like, 'Oh, really?' while inside thinking,

'Remember, whatever they are doing, do the opposite because you don't want to be anything like them.'

I never wanted my brother to die and even now, in a heartbeat, I would swap everything that it taught me just to hear his larrikin laugh again and have the world zing with his unique energy. But going through the grief of his death did, at the very least, show me that in the end, you get there. Even if reluctant, even if the journey itself was an exhausting, difficult, arduous slog, even if it did take a long time, eventually, one day, I would get there. This piece of knowledge was a true pearl because in all the pain and anxiety and stupefyingly weighty grief, there was a small part of me that knew, just knew, that it would one day be not as bad. It was a tiny glimmer, a gleam of hope – and the value of hope should never be underestimated. Hope is often what keeps us going when keeping going seems pointless.

When I was in the first few weeks of bereavement, a friend of mine handed me a phone number of a woman who she knew at work who was reaching out to me. The woman's partner had killed their child a few years earlier and she was generously giving me the opportunity for someone to talk to. I was so grateful that someone who had suffered such a loss was willing to help me, even though my heart broke a little knowing there were others like me out there. But what I really heard was that she was a friend from work. This woman was working! Not only had she found a way to go on but she was employed. I never used that phone number, but its existence nourished a sliver of hope – it meant that mums could survive the loss of their children. They could go on.

Maintaining hope was one step, but I also needed to make some sense of what was going on and give my life meaning.

I'd learnt from my brother's death that I could never really get to the why: 'Why did he die?' 'Why our family?' 'Why did this happen?' They were questions that I worried at constantly, even when occupied with pretty much anything else. Although I'd reasoned out some kind of answers around Neung's state of mind, his choices and so on, I'd never gotten to the (admittedly very self-centred) heart of the 'why' that haunted me in the darkest of moments – why did it have to happen to *me*?

Knowing that there was no real answer to this meant that I didn't agonise over this question again. I knew that there wasn't any inherent meaning in what had happened and that going over and over the events of the past would not help me take the steps I needed to keep going.

I could only imbue my life now with meaning – find some reason to keep on going – because I had learnt that life did just keep going on, and it was up to me how much I engaged with it.

So I'd decided to engage again with life, but it seemed like a fairly dim proposal if there was no real prospect of happiness ever again. I'd learnt, though, that any joy I felt in the process of grief was immediately crushed by guilt. How could I feel joy or laugh or be happy when there was so much loss, so much grief, so much sadness? Didn't joy make a mockery of the loss? But there were moments of happiness, even mirth, right up in the early days of grief that arose just from being around the love and support of family and steadfast friends. One of these friends, when I told him of my feelings of guilt at laughing during a dinner, gave me some advice I've never forgotten: 'The sadness is there, Ing. You don't have to look for it.'

His wisdom helped guide my process of grief away from the wallowing in sadness that I had done for my brother, and more into an active search for bumps of contentment, a savouring of any pleasure and having gratitude, rather than guilt, for any moments of joy that came my way. In my, admittedly rudimentary understanding of the stages of grief, I had always wondered where the feeling okay bit was, and a reassurance that it was okay to feel okay. I became quite determined to seek pleasure and joy – not in an entirely hedonistic way, mind you, but in an authentic way that involved holding onto my values, deepening and nurturing genuine connections with people, giving back as much as I could and noticing, building up and storing the good bits of life. In one presentation, I referred to this last tactic as filling my bucket of sunshine. This doesn't ignore that there are dark days; it's just there in reserve to help.

Even though I was travelling along this way, I was grieving

deeply and needed more than just a search for good bits. I needed to give my life some meaning.

Being right among the agony of grief, it naturally occurred to me that no-one else should have to suffer like we were, and no children should ever die in such a way again. It was a bit difficult to pinpoint what I could do to help prevent such deaths (there was nothing as clear cut as getting cars to slow down in school zones or adding warnings to food packages and so on), although it did irk me that domestic violence didn't command the respect and attention it needed.

Although I hadn't heard of dads killing their kids, I did know that kids were hurt in domestic violence situations and I felt that the police response should have been better when I was first asking them for help in intervening. I'd also worked out that there was no point in scapegoating individual officers.

I wanted to address systemic flaws in dealing with domestic and family violence. Luckily, the police who were assisting me in my case were extremely supportive and I was given the opportunity to address high-ranking officers, firstly through an Asian–Pacific conference, and again on a trip to New Zealand to present to the Commissioner over there.

I then voluntarily spent months travelling throughout Australia, speaking to individual police stations, new recruits and connected services telling them what it was like to be someone trying to use their system. Eventually, my family and I were invited to address the then premier of NSW. Our impassioned plea to take the responsibility away from the woman and instigate further training for all officers around domestic and family violence has been credited with changing the way officers are trained to deal with domestic and family violence.

Although I was honoured to be asked to present, each talk wrenched at me emotionally as I repeatedly described what had happened. I often spent time afterwards deeply affected, experiencing nightmares, anxiety and flashbacks until eventually, I started to decline the invitations in order to take care of myself.

There was another urge within me, though, around dealing with grief. I felt that despite not meeting the criteria for being resilient (I was and am a highly sensitive individual, emotional and not inclined to view my family dying as a 'fortitious challenge'), I was actually surviving, and surviving quite well. I felt that that message needed to be shared, to help challenge the view that to go through something awful means that you will forever be bound in grief. I knew from my own journey that there was a lot of information and views about how to be sad. I wanted to show others how to survive well, despite what they'd been through.

When I was approached to publish a book, I first said 'no', thinking that they wanted a misery memoir allowing people a voyeuristic view into my incredible grief. But when I realised that they wanted my survival story, I agreed to publish and wrote the book *RISE*, published in 2008. Through this and my experience as a trainer, I also wrote and delivered training programs and delivered speeches to thousands of individuals with a focus on building resilience for themselves. In 2012, I was invited to present a TEDx talk. That process and the feedback I received has been an incredible experience.

Having the privilege of meeting so many people has been an unlooked for and extremely gratifying experience. I've shared the stage with incredible luminaries – my own personal heroes in positive psychology and spiritual leaders. So many wonderful people have been in touch with me, talked to me at book signings or after a workshop, often telling me their own heartbreaking stories and telling me that I have inspired them in some way. To hear this is extraordinary, especially when I look back to the person that I was, curled in a foetal position, wishing that I could disappear. I am incredibly grateful for all that I've been able to achieve.

But there has always been a conflict within me. I'd never wanted to be defined as the girl whose brother died and later as the woman whose family was murdered. Yet the very nature of my work, no matter how inspiring, was threatening to make me that person. True, one of my grief grits was that I could never escape from my brother's death or now the death of my family. It would always be a *part* of me, but it didn't have to be the *whole* of me.

In a conversation about victims and survivors, someone once asked me what label I preferred, and I answered 'Ingrid'. I will always be Ingrid first, and my highest motivators in life are not fame and fortune, but, according to the Values in Action survey and my own intuitions, to love and be loved.

Despite what I have been through in my life, I consider myself to be a very lucky person. I have been supported and loved by family and friends, I've had the good fortune to have a medium through which to share my knowledge and learnings, and now the greatest gift of all – a second chance. My life now is full of love with a worthy, funny, respectful and supportive husband and the delight of two children who are frustrating and delightful and gorgeous and fill my bucket of sunshine over and over again.

If I were back, now, in that group with the counsellors, and I'd heard the oyster metaphor, I would probably be more inclined to agree that what I had learnt were pearls. Those little nuggets of knowledge didn't need beauty in order to have value as their guidance proved invaluable in how to navigate through the strange landscape of trauma and grief.

I've always found it confronting when people say that I was meant to go through loss so that I could pass on my knowledge to others. To be honest, I'd rather not have had all that experience. But it is true that going through adversity has taught me a lot, not just about how to grieve, but about how to live.

I've learnt that yes, grief is an arduous slog, but I've also learnt to keep going, because you do get there – not just in the end (as there isn't really an end) but during the journey, too, there are moments of respite, peace and even joy.

I may have learnt that feelings of happiness are followed by guilt, but also that it is the guilt that is the wrong feeling. Happiness needs to be nurtured and built and shared. It is this that makes it all worthwhile.

I have learnt that during times of trouble, people can be

unpredictable and even disappear, but that has taught me to be prepared, to be patient, to choose the ones whose energy I need to be around and to appreciate the ones that stay. I've learnt to accept the love and support and nurturing of others because one day, I will be able to pass that on.

I have learnt that there is no answer to the 'Why?', and no changing the past. So why ask it? And why try to change it? It is much better to focus on the what as in 'What do I do now?'

I've learnt that the world doesn't stop to respect my space, so I need to keep my world to a size that I can handle, limiting outside news and living as much as I can in the days that I have.

I've learnt that I am not immune to further tragedy, but this has taught me to fully appreciate the fragile beauty of life.

I've learnt that staying down is an option, but also that the world has enough victims. I could stay miserable to show my scars or I can love more, be more, help more, share more. I've learnt that scars can be beautiful.

Thoughts and recommendations
Tim Sharp

I knew Ingrid was a special person the first time I met her. And when I first met Ingrid, her trauma was relatively recent so her wounds were still quite raw and, to some extent, unresolved. Yet she presented with incredible calm and control, dignity and quiet determination, humility and courage.

I'm pleased and honoured to say that over the last ten years or so we've become friends. I've also come to be good friends with Ingrid's husband, the equally wonderful Michael, and I'm enjoying watching her two beautiful children grow into lovely little human beings. It's one thing to read Ingrid's story and see her speak impressively on stage, but it's another to see how she lives her life, day in and day out, in the real world. There's no doubt that Ingrid doesn't just 'talk the talk' but also 'walks the walk'.

As a husband and as a parent (let alone as a professional), it's hard for me to imagine anything worse than losing those nearest and dearest to me. I can't possibly comprehend how I'd feel and/or how I'd react. In fact, it's hard to imagine how I'd go on living.

What I do know is that Ingrid is a living and breathing example of how I'd hope I'd be able to cope, and of what's possible when one decides to RISE above terrible circumstances.

As she makes clear when telling her own story, it wasn't easy; and it's still not easy at times. But there are so many great lessons we can learn from Ingrid and her determined resilience that it's impossible not to see her as an inspiration.

- Begin at the beginning and make sure you prioritise what's important – to some extent that's you. This isn't being selfish; it's just being sensible. You can't be happy or healthy or anything positive if you don't first take care of yourself. True, if that's all you did it could be considered selfish, but if you take care of yourself so you can then live a good life, including taking care of others, then that can't possibly be a bad thing.

- Take baby steps. Determine where you'd like to get to (e.g. what your version of health and happiness and thriving and flourishing looks like), develop an action plan and then break that plan down into small, manageable steps. Monitor your progress and reward yourself every step along the way.

- If you don't know what to do then study, learn or find someone who does know what to do (e.g. a professional or a family member or friend) and let them help you.

- Learn how to live; and how to live better. I might be a bit biased because my top strength is a love of learning, but almost all of the people I've met who I'd label as happy or successful or resilient or something similar, all find ways to constantly try to understand themselves and their lives so they can be and live better. This is something Ingrid did and the good news is it's something we can all do.

- Due to the word limits of a chapter contribution to a book like this, Ingrid had to choose what to include and what not to in her story. So although she does briefly refer to it, the version of Ingrid's story you see here doesn't really justice to the incredible support she had from her mother and sister. I've been lucky enough to meet both these people (who also suffered unimaginable loss on that day) and it's not hard to see where Ingrid got at least some of her positive traits. Surrounding yourself with positive people is a constant theme found in all these stories and something we should regularly remind ourselves about.

- One of my favourite aspects of Ingrid's story is when she

refers to the fact that negative life events will always be a part of you, but they don't need to be ALL of you. No matter the size or significance of the trauma or stressor, there's so much value in this important lesson.

- When all seems lost, Ingrid teaches us that not all is lost. As she points out, asking 'Why?' might not always be the right question but in some way or other, finding (or creating) meaning in life IS vitally important. It is, in many ways, the sine qua non (without which there is nothing).

- And finally, find and/or create some meaning in life. We all need a reason to get out of bed in the morning, but it's worth remembering that the meaning will be different for all of us. There's no right or wrong answer! When it comes to self-development recommendations, finding the meaning of life is one of the most common suggestions, BUT it's also almost certainly one of the hardest. In fact, I'm not sure how many people really do ever find THE meaning, but that doesn't mean we shouldn't or can't keep looking for it. You might like to reflect on this quote from Joseph Campbell: 'I don't believe people are looking for the meaning of life as much as they are looking for the experience of being alive.' Find ways to experience being alive and you may well answer your own question!

Learning to share your story
Seb Robertson

Seb Robertson is the founder of Batyr, an organisation that focuses on connecting secondary and tertiary students with speakers on the topics of mental health. When Seb invited me to join the Board of Batyr, I think the expectation was that I would offer my experience and wisdom to help guide him and his young team. I hope I've done some of this, but I can honestly say that I've learnt as much, if not more, from Seb's amazing story and the paradigm-busting work that he and Batyr are doing. They call this reverse-mentoring and I'm so pleased to share with you Seb's chapter because we can all benefit from telling stories and talking more to each other about how we feel.

Over the past four and half years I have embarked on my greatest journey to date. It was, and is, a journey built on vulnerability. At the end of 2010 I decided that I would share my story about my struggles with depression and attempts to take my own life.

I remember when I was around ten years old thinking, 'Wouldn't it be amazing to be asked to write a book?' It wasn't a dream of mine though. I'd pick watching a movie over reading a book any day of the week. And when TED talks came out … ohhh, I was in my element.

Fifteen minutes of absolute gold from absolute strangers

talking passionately about their dreams or discoveries or their hopes. I loved it.

I guess I ruled out writing a book because what on earth would I write about? At ten, I thought if I did, surely it would be about my achievements in the sporting arena. Well, in the last twenty years I can confidently say that I won't be featured in any sport books.

So it is with just a small ounce of disappointment that I am writing this chapter not because of my heroic achievements in battle, or my incredible sporting talents. And not because of my charity bloke appearance in Cleo Bachelor of the Year in 2013. Go ahead and picture whatever you like because it'll be better than the real thing – to be honest I'm pretty happy this isn't a picture book!

I am writing this because I have embraced my vulnerability. For so long I, like so many of us, saw vulnerability as a weakness. It is not a weakness. In the words of author and speaker Brené Brown, 'Vulnerability is the birthplace of creativity, innovation and change.'

It was the decision to embrace my vulnerability that led me to found Batyr. Batyr is named after an Asian elephant in the Soviet Union in the 1960s that was reported to be able to use a large amount of meaningful human speech. Batyr aims to engage, educate and empower young people to speak out about mental health issues by fostering an environment where talking about these issues and getting help is not only accepted but is encouraged and supported. We provide programs that train young people to speak about their personal experiences with mental ill-health and about why and how they sought help and how their story is an example of positive recovery and hope. Stories that are so rarely told in this space.

In 2007, I was fortunate to be living on campus at university at the Australian National University. I was President of John's College. It was a relatively important student leadership role especially for those living on campus. The year was set to be amazing. It was. But it was also one of the most challenging years I've ever had. I broke down internally and fell into a dark hole. It was a space that had no hope, no sense of easing and no solution. Why? Because I didn't talk. Because we didn't talk. Because society wasn't talking. And when we did … it was always about death, about sorrow and about how bad it was. It was never a guiding light to think I could get through this if I just reached out for support. It was never about hope and recovery but always negativity and fear.

I remember the night quite clearly. It was a Thursday night in Canberra, and let's just say I wasn't necessarily sober. I remember so much: the pain of not being able to help one of my closest friends, the pressure of knowing people were watching …

But the thing that stands out in my memory was being tackled to the ground by four or five police officers. Lying on the ground being handcuffed. Tears rolling down my face as I'm picked up and put into the back of the paddy wagon. I was heading to the cop station, and my friend was being taken in an ambulance to the hospital. I remember people being around me but I felt so alone. Again. I remember wanting to be at the hospital to be there with my friend but I couldn't. I couldn't because I'd never helped myself. I never acknowledged that I needed support.

That was my turning point. That was the reason I sought help. It was so that I could continue to help others, but to do that I knew that I had to help myself first. I went on an incredible journey driven by the fact that I could get through it and be there to support, or try to support, my friends and family.

That journey, both the dark one and the recovery, was done in silence. Too afraid of who would catch me using a mental health service and too afraid to admit that I had a mental illness for fear of judgement. After all, I was meant to be a leader. Whatever that means! So the stigma that saw me suffer in silence and drove me to isolate myself in my own pain, in a downward spiral that was akin to falling down a well in slow motion, was the same stigma that stopped me talking about my positive recovery. About how simply being alive was indeed one of my greatest achievements to date.

So I wanted this to change. But how do you create positive behavioural change? How do you connect with someone to the point where they not only acknowledge the challenge of facing a community and potentially themselves, but also recognise that the solution centred around being vulnerable. About opening up and sharing. About allowing others in, so that together, you could get out.

Which brings me back to December 2010. It was then that I decided that I wanted to share my story about recovery with my old school and university college as I felt that it was something that I might have benefited from while I was a student. I didn't want sympathy. I wanted to allow young people to empathise with my experience. I wanted to share my story with young people about my mental illness. I wanted them to know that my simply being here was indeed a success, albeit by chance as opposed to choice, and how it all came from that moment when I embraced the fact that I needed support. It was an idle thought that I never realised would end up changing my life forever.

At the end of 2010 I left General Electric (GE) to pursue a career in ... well, actually, I had no idea. I assumed consulting. All the kids were doing it. When I left GE, I was given a book by my fellow Financial Management Program buddies called *True North*. As *The Wall Street Journal* put it: '*True North* debunks the myth of the superhero top executive ... 125 executives talk about their failures and personal tragedies, and how these setbacks shaped them as leaders.'

A month later I set up Batyr.

I was fortunate to have a great upbringing and a very close family. I continue to gather a lot of inspiration from them, especially my mother who's a legend in her own right, but that's another story.

It's interesting thinking back to how it all started. To be honest, I don't look back that often. I've always viewed looking back as a slowing-down process. Why dwell in the past when we can change the future? I know the past has a huge role in the future – my past led me to pursue change in the education sector around mental health.

I clearly remember one meeting when I was working at GE on their Financial Management Program. It was my first job after graduating with a double degree in Commerce and Economics in 2009. I had lined up this meeting. It only took five months to do it but it was finally game time. It was a tie type of meeting. I love my ties; however, Melburnians don't really wear ties. Apparently that's their style. I agree with it now but at the time I was trying to look powerful. Fake it till you make it, right? Anyway I was stoked I had finally lined up the big meeting.

I walked into the meeting room. I began to sweat, but I was accustomed to that. I'd sweat more because I was nervous that someone would recognise the original sweat and think I was nervous and then that vicious cycle would begin and finally end with me looking as though my arms were strapped down to my body. A challenge I still struggle with to this day!

I'd been in the room plenty of times before but for some reason, this was different. In the room was my boss, who to this day was one of the greatest people I have ever worked for or with, the CFO of GE Corporate and the head of the Financial Management Program, which I was on, and a few other noteworthy individuals.

This was an entertaining affair for them. For me, it meant something more. Like most meetings that I attend where I am fuelled by passion and a strong belief in what I am fighting for, this meant everything. Even I can admit that I probably blew this one up way too much but that mentality, or that commitment, is probably my greatest strength and weakness.

You'd think that after around five months of trying to organise this meeting, it was going to be about something big. It was to get business cards. In the scheme of things I can see how this is very trivial, but to me at the time it wasn't. I get caught up in the little things. I overanalyse. I run through every single outcome of a meeting a thousand times, taking into account reactions, variations, people, and financials – you name it! It can be a great thing but it's also exhausting. I have what you'd probably call a playbook. But just because you have a playbook doesn't mean you can play! For now, I'd rather be playing than coaching or mentoring, but that means I have to be aware of the fact that I'll make mistakes, that there'll always be people on the sideline judging or who have done it differently, better or worse, and that I'll have my personal and professional limitations.

The point is that I pursue something if I believe in it, until I'm told of the result or at least receive a valid explanation. I was told not to bother, to leave it alone, that it wasn't important. It was to me. It gave me some form of identity. I don't know why, but it did and I craved it. Why is it that we are so often fuelled by negativity not positivity? By how we believe people will perceive us as opposed to how we perceive ourselves. The status quo was to just wait until the system gave it to you. I didn't like that and I wanted it changed. So I did. We got those business cards. #Winning.

Those same questions, challenges and advice were, to some degree, the same things I experienced setting up Batyr. It's when you stick your neck out and take a risk that you increase your risk of failure but also increase your chances for success, and positive change and impact. There wasn't a person around me who wasn't supporting me in their own unique way. At times, that's definitely hard to see, but taking a leap of faith into the road less travelled takes courage and a certain level of discomfort. Calculated risk, but risk nevertheless.

That experience definitely symbolised a turning point for me. I realised that I wanted to do more and that if I strongly believed that the outcome was in the best interest of those involved then I'd push to get it changed, regardless of the barriers. It was a trait that was an absolute blessing in disguise in the challenging yet extremely rewarding pursuit of establishing Batyr.

Since setting up Batyr, I have had the fortune of meeting the most amazing individuals and hearing the most incredible stories of courage. I remember sitting at a dinner table recently with some friends from school days and I was sitting next to this girl who I hadn't met before. She asked me what I did so I shared with her my story, and in doing so, she felt comfortable sharing her story with me.

She attended a private school and referred to herself as the average achiever. However, her life took a turn when she left school. She became isolated and turned to heroin; she was addicted for four years. But she got through, she recognised that she needed help and reached out for support services. She has been clean for over four years. It is an incredible achievement, a true act of courage. Yet it's a story not often told. Stories of recovery. Stories of hope. These are the stories that young people need to hear; that we all need to hear. Stories that inspire someone who might be struggling that there is a way through. Stories from peers. And stories encapsulated in an environment that still allow young people to be young. To be playful and to learn.

After embarking on some extensive research I began to realise the severity of mental ill-health in young people. I was not alone in my experiences. In a current Year 12 classroom of 30 students, 7 will have or be suffering from a serious mental health issue. Only 2 of these students will seek professional support, leaving 5 suffering in silence.

In Australia, suicide is the leading cause of death for Australians between 14 and 44. To give that some context, in 2012 there were over 2500 suicides, the largest number recorded in the past ten years. Alarmingly, it is estimated that for every completed suicide in Australia, there are 30 suicide attempts.

So in December 2010, with the support of many individuals, especially family and friends, I set up Batyr to give a voice to the elephant in the room. To engage young people in positive conversations about mental health and empower them to seek help when needed.

I believe there are two big challenges in mental health in Australia. First, the provision of tailored services for every individual in need. There is not going to be a blanket solution to this issue. This challenge needs to be embraced by professionals and the community need to support them to do this. The second challenge is that we need to get people to recognise that they need support. The level of people seeking help in Australia sits at around 25 per cent; we need to create an environment where it is okay to reach out for support. Currently the biggest barrier to help-seeking is stigma and shame.

Mental health research has shown that one of the most powerful ways to create behavioural change around the stigma surrounding mental health is through the sharing of lived experiences from peers.

This is what Batyr does. Batyr provides a safe space for young people to creatively learn how to share their story of mental ill-health. We tell them how their story is the most powerful tool for stigma reduction and ask them to focus on how getting help has helped them, how friends and family and their communities supported them. It is through these lived experiences that we can create the change that we all so desperately need.

We then engage school and university students with these young speakers who have a mental health experience. Through educating young people about the available support networks and systems, students are empowered to reach out when needed.

Batyr was officially launched in August 2011 with one speaker and one story. Since then we have trained over 110 young people who have amazing positive experiences of overcoming mental ill-health. And we've reached over 20,000 young people in schools and universities across Australia. The positive change is happening.

Yet I can confidently say that we are only just scratching the surface. There is still so much ahead of us all. No individual will be able to drive this. We must come together to create a community change. We must create an environment where it is okay to share your story. We must create an environment where it is okay to show your vulnerability.

Batyr is a platform for young people to embrace vulnerability. To learn empathy and to realise that through our shared experiences of overcoming adversity and challenges, we are indeed all courageous. However, Batyr is only what we make it. As my sport coaches will all attest, it doesn't matter how good the coach is on the side of the field, it's the players who determine how they play the game.

Right now we are all the players and we must decide to create the change. We can no longer idly sit by waiting for someone else to take action. To create change. We need a heroic effort and a heroic effort has to be a collective effort. It's imperfect, it's not glamorous. It doesn't suddenly start and end.

It is, most importantly, about courage and vulnerability. It's about following a passion and a cause. It's about creating that dream of change and following it uninvited. Then working with others to make change real.

One of the greatest examples of this that I have experienced has been in the Tamworth community. In 2013 Australia lost a young man called Scotty Campbell. His young wife, Katrina, and an amazing committee of dedicated friends banded together. They decided to create positive change so that their loss and grief, and Scotty's pain, wouldn't be the same for any other young people in the region. In 2014 they organised a huge footy match followed by the White Elephant Winter Ball. It was the weekend of weekends. Great spirits, good community vibe, an open and welcoming atmosphere, and an underlying understanding that we needed change.

The White Elephant Winter Ball, attended by some 500 people, sold out in roughly two weeks. They raised a huge amount of funding for Batyr and since then we have been running programs within the region, reaching more and more young people every month. In 2015 they did it again. As a sign of the amazing work the committee and the Batyr team do, and the wider community's willingness to support this positive change, they sold out again … this time in seven minutes! Five hundred tickets sold in seven minutes. #Legends.

The community wants this change and I hope they are seeing it. The courage and vulnerability of the committee, the service workers, sponsors, guests and all the supporters in Tamworth pulling together like that shows the character of those in the Tamworth and wider community. To dream of creating real change from such a tragedy is nothing but admirable. We have all lost a great man and unfortunately the Australian community loses too many men and women every year. We must change. We must stand together united. We must create a culture that allows us to embrace our own vulnerability.

So now I am at another personal turning point. I have driven Batyr as far as I think it needs me. It's no longer about my story;

it's now one story made up of hundreds and hopefully thousands of personal stories. I have been fortunate to surround myself with absolutely amazing talent and my stepping aside as CEO of Batyr has allowed new leadership and new voices to the table. It's time for me to step aside and support from the sideline. And that I will do. I will cheer, I will be vocal and I guarantee you things will continue to positively change around this stigma.

So how do you finish a story that isn't yet finished? I guess the good news is that it's only a chapter! So here's to the next chapter. Whatever that may hold.

I leave you with some final words from Brené Brown, one of my sources of inspiration:

> If we are going to find our way back to each other, we have to understand and know empathy, because empathy is the antidote to shame. If you put shame in a Petri dish, it needs three things to grow exponentially; secrecy, silence and judgment. If you put the same amount in a Petri dish and douse it with empathy, it can't survive. The two most powerful words when we're in struggle: me too.

Thoughts and recommendations
Tim Sharp

It was early in 2013 and I was interested in helping out a good cause or two. I've always tried to do what I could to offer my skills and experiences, pro bono, to various appropriate charities and organisations.

So I sent out a message via a number of social media networks explaining my situation and asking if people knew of anyone who might be interested in what I had to offer. (For obvious reasons I was focusing mostly on organisations within the mental health domain.)

Relatively quickly, a friend of a friend responded positively, urged me to look into Batyr (about which I knew nothing), connected me online with Sebastian Robertson and invited us to meet up in the real world.

To cut a long story short, we met, got on like a house on fire, and within a few months I'd joined the board of Batyr, which has been one of the best things I've ever done in my life.

I'm a huge fan and supporter of Seb and of Batyr; both are fundamentally changing the landscape of mental health in Australia – for the better!

Why do I think Seb's story is so important? Because as a mental health professional who's worked as a clinical psychologist (and more recently as a consultant and coach), for several decades now I've seen research, and cases, that create in me both hope and concern.

The hope comes from the tremendous advances that have been made in treatment efficacy – psychological, pharmacological and other treatments. In short, we can help most people with the most common problems most of the time, relatively quickly.

But at the same time, my concern comes from the frightening statistic that only about 1 in 4 or 5 of those who need psychological assistance actually seek help. So 70–80 per cent of people with some form of psychological disorder are suffering, often in silence, and not presenting for professional assistance.

Apart from the enormous emotional cost to the individuals, and their family and friends, this also creates an enormous financial burden on our health system and economy generally.

There are many reasons people don't seek help, but one of the most prevalent and most powerful is stigma.

For too long, suffering from an emotional disorder has been considered a form of weakness; too many see seeking help as something that will be embarrassing or worse, something that will negatively impact on their relationships and even employment prospects.

But this has to stop!

Because by not seeking help we're all suffering; and in the worst case scenarios many of us, especially our young men, are dying (suicide is the leading cause of death in young males in Australia).

So what's the answer?

Well, I think Batyr is going to be a big part of the answer – based on his experiences and research, Seb discovered that peer-to-peer sharing of lived experiences – conversations between young people and other young people – significantly reduced stigma and increased willingness and preparedness to seek treatment.

The more we talk about psychological health (and ill-health), the more comfortable we'll be doing something about it. And doing something about it is vitally important as we'll all be affected, either directly or indirectly, at some point in our lives.

So what have I learnt from Seb and his story? I've learnt so much, but some of the highlights are:

- One person can definitely make a difference.
- One conversation can definitely make a difference.
- The benefits of speaking out and sharing stories, being prepared

to be vulnerable and risking potential negative evaluation is definitely worth it (and from ALL the examples I've seen and heard over the years, never as bad as some think it will be).

- Batyr has already helped tens of thousands of young Australians – one conversation at a time, one story at a time.

So what can you do?

- Think about your own personal story, whether mental ill health plays a significant part in that or not, and reflect on what you've learnt from the various ups and downs you've experienced in your life.

- Consider whether or not you could rewrite your story, acknowledging and learning from the less than desirable bits and celebrating and savouring the better and best parts!

- Try to write the story of your life in two or three pages Review it as often as you need to so that it becomes something motivating and inspiring. This doesn't mean you have to deny the negatives or just unrealistically focus on the positives. By all means face up to the cold, hard realities, but face up to them in a constructive way, looking for lessons and growth from difficulties and challenges. And don't forget about the positives. Too often we gloss over these or take them for granted when in fact they should be enjoyed, over and over again.

- And finally, remember the sentiment of Seb's words above: you can't start the next chapter of your life if you keep re-reading the last one.

Putting the pieces back together after PTSD

Allan Sparkes

Allan Sparkes is one of only five Australians in the past 40 years to be awarded the Cross of Valour, Australia's highest decoration for bravery. Allan is also one of only ten Australians to be awarded the Queen's Diamond Jubilee Medal. After twenty years as a frontline police officer, his career ended due to post-traumatic stress disorder coupled with a major depressive disorder, leaving his life in tatters. His recovery involved intensive psychotherapy, medication and determined effort. After years of searching to find himself, he decided to achieve a lifelong goal and rebuild his life, setting off with his wife and two young daughters in a yacht from England and sailing 16,000 nautical miles back to Australia.

'God help me, I was only nineteen.' Do you remember the words to the famous song by the Aussie band Redgum? It describes the life of a young man going to Vietnam and the horrors of war he encountered.

I remember when I was only nineteen and had my first encounter with horror. It was the morning of the Sydney Hilton Hotel bombing, 13 February 1978. I was a young constable in

the New South Wales police force. I had graduated from the
police academy just eight months prior. Here I was, standing on
the awning of the Queen Victoria Building in George Street in
the very heart of the CBD of Sydney. Across the other side of the
street were the remains of a garbage truck. A bomb had blown
it to pieces; its massive steel structure had been ripped apart,
along with the men who had been standing next to it when the
bomb detonated. The fascia of the Sydney Hilton Hotel right
above the truck was covered in blood and gore. A fire engine was
hosing it down and the street gutters were running red.

I was holding someone's hand in my right hand. The hand was
not damaged at all but the wrist was a just a mangled, shredded
mess of flesh, blood vessels and nerve endings. I was looking at
it numbly, looking back and forward at the garbage truck, the
fire engine and then back to the hand. I put the hand in a plastic
bag I was holding; it was starting to fill up with the other parts of
human remains I had been tasked to pick up from the awning.
It was a long way from the shearing sheds I had left not all that
long ago. Back when I was a young, raw-boned country boy,
full of life and laughter. I had been catapulted into a hell I never
thought possible. God help me, I was only nineteen.

Drip, drip, drip. As a street cop, every time you get called to
something terrifying, overwhelming or horrifying, another drip
goes into the bucket. Each drip is a representation of a part of
your soul being removed from your body and dropped into the
bucket. Your fear is that the person you once were can never be
replaced. And that is the way it was. For month after month,

year after year. You think you have seen everything, you think there's nothing left that could shock you, frighten you or horrify you. You become immune to fear and pain. Or so I thought.

On the night of 9 July 1995 my perception of fear and horror was taken to another new level. Two police officers, Senior Constable Robert Spears and Senior Constable Peter Addison has been murdered at Crescent Head on the mid north coast of New South Wales.

'They've been shot, mate, both of them, in the head.' The worst news you can ever receive as a cop. One of your own has been shot dead. This time, not one but two good cops had been murdered. We had to get to the scene and try to help. The two-hour drive from where I was stationed to the command post at Crescent Head seemed like it lasted seconds. One minute we were at our station, getting our gear ready, gathering our shotguns, rifles, radios and vests, running back and forwards from the storeroom to the car. I was thinking to myself, 'Hurry, for God's sake, hurry.' The next minute we were in the command post in this small coastal town. Two good cops lay dead, gunned down attending a routine inquiry. 'There is no doubt he is going to kill more people and kill you if he can,' we were told. 'You have to get to these people before he does.' Time was running out. Tick, tick, tick.

For hours on end, many brave cops went out into the darkness, expecting a bullet to explode into their skulls, ending their lives, as they desperately tried to help those families hiding in their homes. Families frantically seeking somewhere safe to hide before this killer crashed into their homes, looking down the sights of his high-powered rifle at them, killing them all. And all the while, the bodies of these two cops were lying out there somewhere, cold and all alone. There was no help for them; all hope had disappeared like the last breath from their lungs.

We rescued a number of families throughout that night. We saw the sheer unbridled fear on the faces of the little children as we gathered them from their homes and ran with them to safety. It is a horrible sight. Little children, trembling, tears streaming down their face as their mothers try to comfort them, assuring them they are safe. You could tell, though, even when they were safe and surrounded by heavily armed cops in the security of the command post that it was doing little to allay their fears.

And now the darkness was leaving us and the first rays of sunlight were starting to creep over the horizon. The scant cover the darkness of night had given us was gone. With the rising sun, we were much clearer targets now. It was like the gunman had been given an open ticket; take your pick, shoot who you want. We were not in control. In our minds, we were at this killer's mercy. The tightness in our guts was crippling. The next phase of the operation was beginning. More cops and more guns arrived. More commanders, more plans.

Quick, grab a cigarette, suck in that smoke, try to calm yourself. Swap that shotgun for a bigger, more powerful rifle; load up as many bullets as you can, jam spare ammunition into your pockets. Orders are called out, you nod your understanding as you check and double-check your gear. And out you go again.

'Come on, you f— king bastard.' Anger and fear rolling in together. Hatred building for what he has done to your mates, for what he has done to you. 'Take up a position of cover there,' comes the order as fingers point to the street plan. 'Provide covering fire for the entry team.' And down the street you go, finding any cover you can, making your way to your allocated position. The tension is unbearable.

Down on your hands and knees now, shuffling your rifle in front of you, not daring to take you finger away from that trigger. Thinking to myself, 'If I can just get to the end of that fence then I can see exactly where I have to be.' It's just you and your mate. You had already been through so much that night and then you see a policeman lying on his back in the bright light of the morning. 'No, no, no. Please no. Oh please, God, no.' Green grass, blue sky, upturned black boots, blue pants, blue shirt. Red where there should be blue. NO, there should not be blood on that shirt. No, please. Blood. Bob. No, PLEASE. Blood, blood, blood. Stillness. Not a sound except the screaming in my brain. I could not comprehend what I was seeing. This could not be real.

'Police, Police, Police!' The screams of the entry team as they crashed through the killer's house cut through the silence. I caught a vision of upturned boots, someone else lying on their back. Friend or foe? Mate or killer? The amateurish attempt at creating camouflage clothing, the camouflage paint on the rifle, the two magazines taped together in preparedness for a firefight were the first clues. What was left of his head was the next. The killer was no longer a threat.

But where are you, Pete? I had known Pete for over ten years. I had been his instructor at the Detectives Training Course. My wife had been in his class as well. We had shared many great times with him. Oh dear, God, no. Hour upon hour of adrenaline-fuelled fear and horror had taken their toll. I felt a numbness I had never experienced before in my life. I wanted to cry as I sat down with Pete, I wanted to feel something to ease this agony. I am crying now as I remember my friend lying dead beside me. I did not want to leave my friend. I just wanted to stay with him and care for him. I was frightened to stand up for if I fell over, I felt as though I could never stand up again. In the end, I just wanted the wind to pick me up and blow me away. Drip, drip, drip.

'Help! Please help me! Help me, please help me!' My mind and my life started to descend into a darkness I had never known before.

Just a few months later, the descent into darkness took on a new form of reality. It was 3 May 1996. An eleven-year-old boy was playing in a flooded creek in Coffs Harbour on the north coast of New South Wales when suddenly he was sucked down into a stormwater pipe full of cold, filthy, flood water.

Have you ever heard a child screaming for their life? This child had been swept 600 metres down this flooded stormwater pipe. Six hundred metres in the pitch black, in freezing cold water, being tumbled over and over in a narrow concrete pipe. It was literally a roller-coaster descent into unimaginable hell. My police partner Gavin Dengate and I had shared that hell trying to find him. We had plunged into those pipes again and again, searching desperately for this child in the labyrinth of narrow pipes deep below the ground. We were racing desperately against time and the elements. It only had to rain one more time and things would turn deadly, for all of us. There had already been five days of torrential rain and every waterway was at absolute saturation point. I was praying harder than I had ever prayed in my life. 'Please, God, don't let him get washed away; please don't let him get washed away.' I was also hoping like hell that the pause in the rain would hold out. Tick, tick, tick.

Michael Marr, a paramedic, plunged down into the drain system to help as I crawled up the pipe, not much wider than my shoulders. My fingernails and toenails tried to gain some grip against the water flowing down against me as the screams followed the water down in my direction, getting louder and louder, more and more desperate. 'Please, help! Help! Please help!' The volume of my screams back at him seemed to be lost in the noise and mayhem. Maybe I wasn't screaming at all, maybe I just thought I was. Dear God, where is this child? I was pleading with this child in my head, 'Please stop screaming, mate, please stop.'

Suddenly, in my torchlight, I saw something – a little face. Only the face, so white it was like the face of a tiny ghost. I was yelling to him, 'Hang on, mate! I'm coming, I'm coming!' He was still quite a distance from me and as I got closer, in the beam of the torchlight, I could see Jai was hanging onto a piece of timber wedged across the pipe. I was about 30 metres up the pipe and 3 metres under the roadway.

'Jai!' I screamed. 'Come to the light. Let go of the timber and come to the light.' I was exhausted and my fear of his being washed away was getting stronger. I was still clawing forward but I was slowing. 'Jai, Jai! Mate, let go of the timber. Come to the light, Jai.'

I had hardly anything left. Jai seemed so close but I had no energy to go on. I was becoming terrified at the thought of more rain and that we were both going to drown down that pipe. I did not want to go through that feeling of being submerged by flood water again with no way out. Finally, Jai let go of the timber and I saw him coming towards me. *Oh my God, oh my God*, I was saying to myself. *I've got him. He's going to be safe.*

'Mick, I've got him!' I screamed down the pipe. 'Mick, I've got him.' Jai washed into me and I folded him up in my arms. 'You say thank you, God,' I said. 'Thank you, God,' he said in this little frail voice, shaking uncontrollably. He started to sob and my emotions overtook me. I held onto him, crying with him.

About an hour later water was cascading over me again. This time it wasn't filthy cold flood water, it was steaming hot clean water from the showerhead above me. I was curled up on the floor of the shower recess, sobbing. The fear and trauma of what I had experienced in those pipes, mixed with the exultation of saving this child, was too much for me to cope with. My darling wife Deb came in and held me in her arms. My life and my mind were starting to fall apart. Drip, drip, and now my bucket was starting to overflow. In the following months, my life spiralled into the hell of PTSD and chronic depression. I had become suicidal.

It was the morning of 4 October 1996. My attempts the previous night to hide from the demons and dreadful visions had failed. I thought that staying awake for as long as I could, drinking scotch, would shield me. But when I eventually fell into a restless, brief sleep, the lurid visions returned. When I woke, I turned over and looked over at Deb. She lay there, sleeping quietly, peacefully, far removed from the torture inside my head. The tears welled in my eyes. I got out of bed and went to my little girl, Nikki, and kissed her as she slept in her room. I vowed they would be safe. No matter what it took, I would make sure they were safe. In my shattered mind, I thought the best way to ensure that was to take myself out of the equation.

I went to work, planning how I was going to end my life. I was sitting there in that deep, dark place in my mind when my thoughts were interrupted by the intrusion of a workmate.

'What are you doing, mate?' he asked with a quizzical look on his face.

Instead of answering, I stood and handed him my gun that I had been holding in my hand, contemplating my last moments of life.

'Are you okay, mate?'

'No mate, I'm f – ked, I just need to get home. Can you call Deb and get her to come home?'

It took all my energy just to stand up. I wanted to drop to the floor and curl up in a ball. I was feeling so ashamed and humiliated. I had failed and I was no good to anyone anymore. I was Humpty Dumpty and I had fallen off the wall, shattering into a thousand pieces. It was going to take more than all the king's horses and all the king's men to put me back together again.

The following morning I was with my GP, Dr Oliver. I sat in his surgery, sobbing uncontrollably with Deb by my side, feeling like a total failure. Doc Oliver obviously saw that I was in a critical state and arranged for an immediate consultation with the resident psychiatrist at the Base Hospital Mental Health Unit. I remember him saying, in his beautiful Scottish accent, 'It'll be all right, old son. It will be all right, old son, just hang in there.'

In the office of the resident psychiatrist, I sat in the chair with Deb beside me, and could not stop crying. It became clear that I was a whisker away from suicide. The psychiatrist was very matter of fact. He asked me if deep in my heart I really wanted to live or die.

'I want to live,' I said through my clenched teeth, wretched tears streaming down my face, 'but what if I hurt Deb and Nikki? I'm f – king terrified I'll hurt them. I'm going out of my f – king mind.'

I wanted to stand up, scream and scream at the top of my lungs, rip myself to shreds with my bare fingernails, find a knife and plunge it into myself over and over – anything to get at these unspeakable feelings inside me, to destroy them any way I could.

I remember that I started to plead for help, something that I had never done before. 'Please help me, for God's sake, please help me.' I could hear these words repeated over and over but I don't know if I was actually speaking them or if I was just hearing them. Inside my head I was screaming in the agony of unimaginable anguish and desperation. I was petrified that I was going mad. Somehow the psychiatrist sensed what I was thinking.

'Al, you are not going mad. You have some serious illnesses and we are going to make you better. It is not uncommon for people in the state you are in to have these feelings or these visions. You are very unwell and we are going to make you better.'

The psychiatrist immediately prescribed antidepressants and an antipsychotic drug. The psychiatrist told us that this drug was an extremely strong sedative and should allow me to sleep and not do much else. It was going to deter me from causing any harm to myself or anyone else as it prevented me from forming any harmful intent. For two weeks I was just a shell of a man. I could do little but sleep, sleep and sleep. It was such a *deep* slumber without the visions, a great relief from my mental torture. The drugs held the demons at bay.

My only physical activity was walking down to the edge of the beach. The decisions I could make were to brew a coffee now and again, and light a cigarette. I would sit on a seat at the edge of the beach for hours on end, staring out across the ocean. I was mesmerised by the motion of the waves continually rolling onto the beach. The sound of the water was calming. My focus on the waves on the shore broadened further out to sea and the horizon. It was infinity. I started to imagine being on a yacht, setting the sails for the east and sailing off forever, never turning back, never stopping, just getting further and further away from all the horror.

I continued with the antidepressants and was having three sessions a week with the psychiatrist. The diagnosis of chronic post-traumatic stress disorder coupled with chronic depression was confirmed. My psychiatrist was based in the Jordan Centre, the psychiatric unit of the local base hospital. The Jordan Centre was also the local methadone clinic so there was a mixture of heroin addicts and people with varying degrees of mental illness in the waiting room. So here I was, the local detective, keeping company with addicts I had arrested plus the people who, not so long ago, I had been happy to refer to as the local loonies. I had taken the express lift from the penthouse to the shithouse. I hated this place. Every time I approached the building I felt like turning around and going away, it didn't matter where to. It was as if each time I went there I was admitting I was worthless. But I knew that if ever I was going to get better, I had to keep going through those doors. I had no pride left to swallow.

Yet out of that horrible place, life eventually took me on another journey to a very magical place. But that journey did not take weeks, or months. It took years of hard work and determination to get well again, to regain my life, my marriage, my relationship with my children and my sense of worth. I had realised my sense of worth was like a life-support system; I had never fully realised what it would mean to get it back.

And so, with Deb, my fourteen-year-old daughter Nikola, and my nine-year-old daughter Alayna, I headed off on a journey that would change my life and theirs as well. In 2009 we purchased a yacht. A yacht capable of taking us across those oceans I had once imagined I was sailing on. Back in those deep dark times of years gone past. Our yacht was called *Sunboy* and she was the finest yacht I could ever imagine owning. Where did we purchase this magnificent vessel? Sydney? Brisbane? Melbourne? No, none of the above. Our yacht *Sunboy* was tied up safe and sound in the Hamble Point Marina on the south coast of England. In March 2009 the four of us boarded a plane in Sydney and with one-way tickets, set off for a new life at sea.

In those early days of living on board our *Sunboy*, our most adventurous plans were to sail 72 nautical miles across the English Channel to France. From there, we hoped and dreamed of developing the skills, confidence and belief we might, just might, be able to sail her all the way into the Mediterranean Sea, a distance of about 600 nautical miles. But, like all life plans, changes took place and fate played a little hand. In November 2009, along with another young crew member, our dear young friend from Australia Luke Reeves, my family and I set sail from the Island of Las Palmas in the Canary Islands for the Caribbean Islands, 3000 nautical miles across a very large and unforgiving ocean. We had decided to throw all of our previous plans out the window – we were embarking on an adventure that we hoped (and prayed) would take us all the way back to Australia.

We made it across the Atlantic Ocean, not without our dramas, but we always felt as if we were in control. Often at night, I'd look at whoever was on the helm, sailing the boat by the feel of the wind and the sea. I would see a picture of concentration, a face glowing from the red light of the compass used to help steer their course. I was in awe. The level of ability and confidence of every member of this crew had soared. It was like I could read their minds sometimes, and I believe deep in their own hearts they had developed a new-found self-belief. Deep in my heart, I believed their dreams and ambitions could be as endless as the skies and the oceans we were sailing on.

Eventually we found ourselves in the magical Galapagos Islands getting ready to tackle our next major nautical obstacle, sailing across the world's largest ocean. It was another 3000 nautical mile-plus passage until we made landfall in the French Marquesas Islands.

This was the part of the trip that really did it for me. There was one day in particular where it all came together, where I'd overcome the horrors of my life. It was appropriate I was in the cockpit, all alone, my family and Luke sleeping peacefully down below. Standing on my boat and looking back over the stern at the rising sun; the wake of my boat leading to a golden ball coming up over the eastern horizon reinforced my sense of achievement. I stood there, allowing myself to remember sad times from the past. I bundled them up and threw them over Sunboy's stern, letting them float free and drift away. My fear of failure was drifting away with them. I turned and looked forward to the bow, to the full moon setting over the western horizon. I could see a better future, better than any I had known before.

For me, the Pacific Ocean passage was the most significant part of our whole trip. What an experience. How many places in the world can you be where you do not see another human being for seventeen days straight? I saw only the lights of two fishing ships far off in the distance in that time. Apart from that, no-one else saw any sign of humanity. Our only contact with the outside world, if we needed it, was our satellite phone. No ships, no other sailing boats, no planes, nothing. On the one hand it is as if you are the tiniest speck of life imaginable, but on the other, you have this incredible feeling that all the world is yours. It was the most beautiful bloody sensation you could imagine.

About 5 pm on 8 June 2010, seventeen days after setting out from the Galapagos Islands, we dropped anchor in the harbour of Nuka Hiva, French Marquesas, having logged just over 3100 nautical miles. It was our second and longest ocean passage.

Arriving in Nuka Hiva did not give me a sense of relief so much as an enormous sense of triumphant achievement and recovery. How sweet that feeling was. For many years I did not hold a whole lot of hope that life was ever going to get back to where I wanted it to be, but I was determined to try my guts out to get there. I could now stand tall and proud again. This passage had resurrected my old self but even better than that, it created a new and better self. It made me realise that my whole life's journey had been worth it.

I knew that these positive feelings were going to continue and I was going to make sure I enjoyed every single one of them, not just on the journey back to Australia but every day I could after that.

Who could blame me for having tears well up in my eyes as we took our final turn to starboard, turning past Mutton Bird Island and into our home port of Coffs Harbour. We had made it – 16,000 nautical miles from where we had started out so long ago and so far away. The emotion of getting my boat and family home safe and sound is difficult to put into words. Nothing seems to be able to describe it adequately. At that moment, I could never imagine any greater accomplishment. Finally, I could stand tall and proud once more, truly believing in myself. All the king's horses and all the king's men had done their job well. Allan Sparkes was back together again.

Thoughts and recommendations
Tim Sharp

One of the decisions I regularly face, when finding myself on the program of a conference or event, is whether or not to arrive early to see speakers presenting before me and/or whether or not to stay back later for those coming after me. Most of the time, this decision is made for me due to other commitments or travel arrangements, but sometimes it's just one I have to make depending on the individual(s) or topics. Some decisions are definitely easier to make than others.

One of the easier decisions I've had to make was when I discovered I was speaking on the same program as Allan Sparkes at an event for several hundred NSW school principals. I'd vaguely heard of Allan, but the short bio and presentation overview in the program strongly piqued my interest and so it was that I returned to the event, the day after I'd spoken, to listen to his remarkable story.

I was blown away. I've heard many amazing stories but I was so impressed with Al's courage and resilience and honesty and humility; with his determination and his perseverance and very much with his desire, in recent years, to help others.

I pride myself on always trying to learn something from every situation I'm in and from every person I meet. Learning from Al and his story was not hard at all. As I hope you think too, there's so much value in what he's been through and even more importantly, how he's dealt with it.

It goes without saying that each and every one of you is different, is living a different life in different circumstances, and so each and every one of you will interpret Al's story in a way that makes sense to you. None are right or wrong. What I learnt from the impressive Mr Allan Sparkes was how it takes courage to seek help, but that when you do, recovery and rehabilitation is possible.

For a variety of reasons it's not always easy to seek help, and this is especially true in the workplace in which Al had spent pretty much all of his adult life. There's no doubt things are improving, but I don't think it's inappropriate to note that back when Allan experienced his trauma, the police force didn't necessarily provide as much assistance to its troops as it could have.

Thankfully for Al, and for all of us, he did find a way to seek help, which leads me to the second thing I learnt from Al's story: perseverance is required in order to make the most of therapy. As you'll see from many of the stories in this book, therapy (in its various guises) is often very effective. Most people will get better from most problems. But many people will not necessarily find the best treatment or treatment provider for them the first time they try.

Some do, and that's great. But for a significant proportion of people who suffer, it might be the second or third or even fourth or fifth person or treatment that ultimately provides relief.

And the important message for all of us is, 'Don't give up!' Keep trying different approaches and styles from different people (the only caveat being, in my opinion, that what you try should be evidence based and offered by appropriately qualified professionals). Although I very much believe that proven treatments are and will be effective because of their active ingredients, I also believe that the very act of trying and persevering is powerful in and of itself, and provides the person trying with hope, optimism, confidence and more.

I have no doubt that however powerful the various treatments Al tried ultimately were, one of the most important variables was the love and support and patience of his wife. Having a supportive person – an intimate partner or good friend or family member – is an amazing asset. Another lesson I learnt from Al is how important it is to allow these people into our lives so they can help us. Many of us have loved ones who are prepared to help – if only we let them. But too often we push them away or we're afraid to let them see us in our distressed and vulnerable state so we struggle on alone – miss out on the powerful benefits that can come from these wonderful people.

So Allan sought help, he persevered, he allowed others to love and to help him but notably, he also showed tremendous courage to take a risk and pursue his dream! Imagine being in the state he was in after all he'd been through and then deciding to sail around the world, having never done anything even remotely close to this previously!

Not all of us will have such a goal, or even a dream that requires taking such a massive (yet calculated) risk. But all of us do have something we've always dreamed of doing and for many of us, real happiness will come when we have the courage to pursue these dreams. Otherwise we live on with regrets that can eat away at our contentment and undermine our attempts to be satisfied with life. I've spoken to Al about what it took to do what he did; and it took a lot. But there's no doubt at all that the return on investment was massive and that the risk was definitely worth taking.

And finally, what impresses me so much about Al has been his desire and commitment to give back, help others and do what he can to ensure that when and where possible, others don't suffer the way he did. Through his speaking and writing and work with beyondblue, Allan has undoubtedly helped hundreds if not thousands of others to overcome adversity and live better, more fulfilling lives.

And so from this story, and from the lessons I've pulled out, I encourage you, now, to consider the following and put into practice any and all that are relevant to you:

- Consider whether or not you need to seek help. It might be for your psychological health, but it might also be for your physical health and wellbeing, your relationships, finances or any other area of your life. And don't think you need to be absolutely desperate to seek help. If you're in any way less than satisfied with any aspect of your life then find the most appropriate expert and get in early!

- Don't be afraid to seek a second opinion, or to try a different provider if for whatever reason you don't gel or agree with the first person you see.

- Learn to let other people into your life. Let them love and support you. It's okay to need help; we all do sometimes. Not accepting support will only make things worse for all involved.
- Consider taking some risks. John F Kennedy once said, 'There are risks and costs to action. But they are far less than the long-range risks of comfortable inaction.' Imagine if you went for your dream; imagine if you didn't!
- If you are considering pursuing your dream or a significant, long-term life goal, break it down into small, manageable steps. Al didn't just buy a boat and sail around the world without any planning. Neither should you necessarily embark on a major project without the necessary preparation. But with the right sort of work and learning and appropriate training, you can almost certainly achieve far more than you ever thought possible!
- And finally, look for ways to give back and to help others. In giving we receive.

'It ain't weak to speak'

Sam Webb

Sam's story is the epitome of mateship in the best possible way. Sam suffered a tremendous loss when one of his best mates committed suicide, but he has been able to turn this into an uplifting story of hope and optimism. Light can come from dark and Sam went on to co-found the charity organisation LIVIN, which is now working to help others realise that 'it ain't weak to speak'.

A smile that could light up a room, a persona that would instantly create positive hope to the saddest of sad, and a giving hand that not even some of our closest friends could comprehend were just some of the traits my best mate Dwayne Lally made his own. That was until the darkest of mornings on Sunday 15 September 2013, when life was no longer an option for him – and LIVIN was established in the wake of the most tragic of circumstances.

It was like a bomb had landed. Everyone who was touched by Dwayne in some way was left critically injured with scars that would last a lifetime, asking questions as to the whys, what ifs, could be's. Life had changed forever and what we knew up until then was no longer important. It was what we did after that morning that would symbolise his life and legacy. And so we did.

Firstly, let's go back a few years. Dwayne and I encountered each other on the football field when we were seven years of age on the Gold Coast. He played for our arch rivals the Redbacks with Casey Lyons (Dwayne's best mate). I was playing for the Bears. Both Dwayne and I were among the most competitive in our ages, and to this day I still smile and laugh at the thought of our banter on and off the field. No matter what it was we would do, everything was a competition, a fierce battle for first versus second. On most occasions I would come off second best. Dwayne was a very talented young man at almost anything he tried. I wouldn't feed his ego, though, as he didn't need it. He was a very confident and outgoing kid who was just naturally amazing at whatever he did. That was just Dwayne; he had the gift!

We both went to different schools growing up, playing both against and alongside one another in our representative teams in both rugby league and touch football. We had a rare friendship: we were not always together and hanging out, but regardless of how much we spoke or saw each other, things never changed. Every time we saw one another we just picked up from where we left off and that was the beautiful thing about Dwayne. No matter where you went or what you did he was just sincere, true and genuine. Qualities like this are extremely hard to find in people and I will cherish that about him for the rest of my life. In my eyes, that is a true mark of friendship, and something I still can't accept no longer exists for me.

I fast forward now to 2013, a year that started off absolutely terribly for me. To be brutally honest, though, I brought it on myself. I had made poor decisions due to my very impulsive nature and my inability to take no for an answer. I packed my bags and headed home from the USA where I had been living and dating a girl for five years, merely three months off antidepressants. I had been diagnosed with depression and anxiety when studying for my bachelor's degree in Finance in 2009.

Mental illness was already something that was close to me and my family, having lost family members and very close friends to suicide before. It is something I have learnt to accept exists and something I saw people pay the ultimate price for having. I wasn't in a good headspace and so was in and out of work, lost a ton of money taking stupid risks, and drank excessively to the point where drinking was my way out, my way of feeling good about myself, or so I thought in the moment.

Before I knew it, I had been boozing and chasing highs for the better part of six months. Then rolls around September 2013. It was like I clicked my fingers and time just flew by; it was just one big blur. I will admit, though, that some of my best memories were made that September, ones that will stay with me forever. Ones I wish I could relive again and again and again.

It was the month the Gold Coast Rugby League finals took place, when Dwayne, a massive group of our friends and I piled in to watch my brother and close mates play in the grand final at Burleigh Heads, Pizzy Park. My brother's team was victorious that day and we were all made sure of this by Dwayne's chanting from the sidelines, 'The better Webb, The better Webb!', which got the crowd on their feet and energies raging. The atmosphere was electric. You just had to be there to witness it. He was great at this. It was his trademark. I will never forget that day ...

Dwayne had planned a double date for me to go on with him, his girlfriend and her good friend (I won't mention her name but she knows who she is) two weeks later. A night of some nice wine, good food and of course great chat was planned. That was something you could almost always guarantee would happen when we got together. We would compete on who could be the loudest, funniest and more charming. That was just what we did. We loved the banter. We would always find ways to laugh and entertain ourselves in pretty much any situation we were in. I guess that's why we got along so well. His energy and ways of making a dull moment one to remember were something I think a lot of people were drawn to. It was contagious.

Instead, the double date was scrapped. Dwayne had other plans. He decided to throw a bit of a barbecue at the place he was renting with some other good friends of ours. It was okay with me either way – Dwayne wanted to do that, so I was happy. A late shift in plans was always on the cards for Dwayne; he was very spontaneous and I loved that about him. He arranged for the girls to pick me up that night and we drove over to Dwayne's place around 8 pm on Saturday, 14 September.

We arrived at Dwayne's place around 8.15 pm and were loudly and proudly welcomed by the man himself. I will never forget that bear hug he greeted me with on his doorstep and his crazy dress sense – something I respected, and something he could pull off extremely well. On this occasion it was rolled-up shorts with Converse high tops, a purple striped tank top with a T and C logo in the centre and an oversize beanie pulled back enough to keep his fringe out. Dwayne rushed us in and ensured we were quickly comfortable and made sure we were welcomed with open arms. This was nothing out of the ordinary; that was just Dwayne, he put you first. Footy was on, music was a tad louder than you would normally expect at this time of the evening, but we were all having a great time. There were about ten of us at this stage of the night. A couple of hours had past, a few more people had entered the premises; it was becoming more like a party now, the music was louder and it was on. Dwayne called me into his room that night between 10.30 and 11 pm, closed the door and locked it behind me.

The first thing Dwayne said to me was, 'I consider you one of my best mates, Webb, and this is why I am telling you this.' He opened up to me about everything that night. Things that caught me so off guard that I didn't even see coming. He described some of his extreme lows, the Lithicarb (a type of medication he was prescribed at the time), the internal battles he continually had with his own mind for no particular reason; these were just some of the things that were spoken about inside his room that night. I was aware that Dwayne had suffered from bipolar disorder for quite some time, but I wasn't sure to what extent because he hid it so well. I will never forget when he said, 'Webb, you know I have tried to hang myself before. I am the sort of guy that would actually do it.'

There was dead silence for a couple of seconds – it felt like a lifetime – until he straightaway reassured me that he was in the best headspace of his life at this point in time. I was completely and utterly in shock. I couldn't even properly comprehend what I had just been told. The happiest man, who would light up an entire city, had just told me that he had tried to take his own life before. Not once but twice. I was trying my best to hold back my tears but they were clearly evident. I looked at Dwayne and said, 'Bro, you aren't alone. No matter how hard life is, I will always be there for you. Even if I am going through my own problems I will do my best to make sure you're okay. You can call me anytime you want, bro, I will be there for you.'

I could see Dwayne getting a little moved by this whole situation and just how confronting this whole ordeal was for the both of us. We had both lost friends to suicide before and knew the profound impact it had on so many lives around you. It was just outrageous to even consider that this was an option for Dwayne.

My head was in an absolute chaotic race as to what to say next. I was asking myself questions as to what I would like to hear if I said this to my best mate. I'm not a psychologist, I am not a doctor by any means, but I have great ears and I'm good at listening.

So I listened more than ever to Dwayne that night. I also said everything I thought I knew best to say in this situation. I reassured him he was loved, he had so much support around him and there were so many people that would give anything to make him happy. At one point I was actually resonating with how he had felt, a feeling I could relate to from my past experience, and so I let him know that too. I reiterated that he wasn't alone and that it is okay to ask for help.

Dwayne being Dwayne brushed aside any concerns and carried on like nothing had happened. He promised me that night that he would never do something so silly again. Those were his exact words. He said to me, 'I have the best family, I am happy at work, and life is great right now, but that's how I have felt in the past, so I just wanted to let you know.'

I do remember particularly well him thanking me for being there and listening to him, without judgement, and actually understanding what he had gone through. Everything was perfect and just the way he wanted it to be, he said. 'We're going to the top, Webb!' he said with a smile from ear to ear! This was a figure of speech Dwayne and I had made up one day. The top was the best place to be in life. A place where great things happen. I look back now and I can see it clear as day; Dwayne's grin was so deceiving. He was very good at masking his true emotions.

An outsider looking in on Dwayne's life would think he had it all. An amazing family bond, a great job, a great personal life. But I guess all of this doesn't matter when your mind is not right. We both left his room after about 30 minutes, in good spirits, and a bit of old school banter proceeded to take place again. This was a given when we were together.

After Dwayne had just completely opened up to me and told me what most of his closest friends and family didn't even know, I was keeping a watch on his movements from that moment. I did this because someone who suffers from a mental illness can change at the drop of a hat – even over the smallest things – and speaking from experience, they act on emotions not on logic.

That night, not long after we spoke, Dwayne was having a discussion with his girlfriend. She came running out crying to me after a small argument had broken out between the two of them. I knew he hadn't come out the front door. So I scrambled around the house looking for him, hoping he was out the back. Dwayne wasn't in the house at all. He had snuck out the back door and around the side of the house to his car. By the time we got to the front of the house he was long gone. I called his mobile phone frantically and sent numerous text messages one after the next, begging for him to come back. I sent one text that said: 'Brother, I love you. Please do not do anything we had spoken about tonight. I am here for you, bro, everything will be ok I promise.' But no reply, no response. His phone was still ringing, but he wasn't picking up.

I drove halfway around the Gold Coast that night looking for him, trying to maintain my positive thoughts and reassuring everyone that he would be okay. My hope started to wain after he didn't answer calls from his mum. This is when I really started to panic. Dwayne was a family man; he was extremely close to his entire family, something people would envy. If he wasn't picking up his mum's calls, it wasn't a good sign at all. Dwayne and his mum, Kym, were as close as they get.

By this time it was around 2 am the morning of 15 September 2013. I lay awake that whole night wondering where he could be.

After our discussion in his room that night I couldn't help going over hundreds of different scenarios in my mind. I hoped and prayed that he was safe and okay. This was the day Dwayne and I were supposed to watch the Floyd Mayweather and Canelo Alvarez fight down at the local bar. Dwayne was an avid boxer and very good at it.

It was the slowest day in history and concentration levels didn't exist. All we wanted to do was find Dwayne. I remember one of the boys putting up his picture online and a message saying, 'If you see our brother let us know ASAP.' We finally made the call to lodge his disappearance with the police as it was now twelve hours since he'd gone and we still had no clue of his whereabouts. The day had a really weird, empty feel about it. You know when you know something isn't right. You sense it. The air was different; it was just bizarre.

My phone rang at around 5 pm that afternoon and it was the call I never wanted to receive. 'Webby, Dwayne's dead man, he was found hanging from a tree in Tallebudgera. I can't believe this is true.' My whole body left me momentarily and I couldn't even begin to believe this was happening. I was completely speechless until I broke out into a cry; one that was almost silent. I just couldn't believe this had happened. My best mate, Dwayne, who opened up to me only a few hours before this, is dead. Gone.

The effect of Dwayne's passing on his family and friends, people who I care so greatly for, was just devastating. I needed to do something to help. I wanted to turn a negative into a positive. I wanted to make a positive change. The loss of Dwayne Lally changed a lot of people's lives forever. Casey Lyons, Dwayne's and my best mate, sat down with Dwayne's family shortly after. Dwayne wouldn't have liked his death to be in vain, so we decided to come up with a clothes label called LIVIN. We would sell shirts to raise awareness for mental health and suicide prevention.

Dwayne used to always say, 'We're livin, man, we're livin!' And that's where the name LIVIN was born from. The arrow inside the word LIVIN came from our favourite saying, 'We're going to the top'. So it all made perfect sense and it was something close to all of us. I know Dwayno would have liked the concept behind it too. He was always into his fashion, so this was something we needed to continue after his departure and so we did. To make our statement even stronger, one of the boys came up with the tag phrase, 'It ain't weak to speak'. This fitted perfectly with our philosophy so we added that to our T-shirts and the label took off.

By this stage I had left my full-time job. For the very first time in my life I was passionately pursuing what I wanted to do; help people. Thankfully Casey and I had some pretty established connections on the Gold Coast so we launched our website and started getting noticed in the local community for the work that we were doing.

I know why the label started to take off and it wasn't because of the name LIVIN – it was much deeper than that. It was the story behind it. It was this whole other world that we unlocked and gave a voice to; gave hope to. Mental illness is something that relates to almost all of us in some way and people wanted to be a part of the family. They wanted to unite. Because of the love and support we got from the community and all of our supporters, we started growing faster than we ever imagined. Soon we were rolling out various men's and women's clothing ranges and later started our social media pages. The pages starting gaining traction immediately and they haven't slowed down since. And because of the support, we are now able to help change the lives of many people who we once thought we couldn't reach.

We kept plugging away selling merchandise online and attending some local events on the Gold Coast for about a year as a means of raising awareness and funds for the cause. We later teamed up with Headspace, a national registered charity organisation for youth and mental health, to do some work. This gave LIVIN more credibility and allowed us to partner with some bigger events where we reached a bigger audience. We were getting such good feedback and responses from the public that Casey and I discussed the possibility of transforming LIVIN into a fully registered charity.

A couple of months prior to this I met a girl at a mate's place, who introduced us to the law firm Minter Ellison. We pitched our ideas to them and they decided to work pro bono for us. This would allow us to get our legal work sorted and after six months of gruelling paperwork and back and forth applications with the Australian Taxation Office, we finally got the greenlight we were so anxiously waiting for. Top LIVIN was now a fully registered charity for mental health and suicide prevention. This milestone was a very special day for us. And a lot of emotions were felt that day.

This was the beginning of something far bigger than we had once anticipated. We were about to set off into the great big world with a charity that had formed a united family. A charity that we hope changes the way people perceive, understand and interpret mental health. A charity that changes the way people think. A charity that gives people hope and confidence when they need it most.

I know Dwayne has been on this entire journey with us. There is not a day that goes by when we do not think about him in all that we do. We will carry his legacy on and we will be forever grateful for the times that we spent with him. Our job is far bigger now. We have lives to save and people to give hope to. This is something Dwayne knew by second nature. He was a very giving person. Each time I look at LIVIN I see Dwayno smiling with his great big pearly whites. I would trade in LIVIN for Dwayne's life in a heartbeat, but that is just not possible. We have to live with what's done and we hope that by turning a negative into a positive, people can truly see why LIVIN is what life is all about.

Now we are looking at getting involved with schools and universities, sporting clubs and the corporate sector and rolling out a program to give people insight into our mantra and philosophy – 'It ain't weak to speak'. We aim to be involved in events and spread our message not just in Australia but globally. If we can rewrite the footprint on mental health and change the dynamics in which it exists, we will save many people's lives.

We currently ship worldwide and orders are growing astronomically thanks to all of our amazing supporters. Our immediate plans are to roll out a full health and fitness clothing and merchandise range for both men and women. This will likely be our main source of fundraising so we can continue in our relentless mission. Our overall goal is to get people to accept that mental health is no different than a broken arm or cancer. It is an illness that can be beaten. An illness that you should be able to speak openly about without being judged, embarrassed or looked down on. Being able to speak about your true feelings without being criticised or humiliated is the most important part of living in a world that will embrace this change and we are here to promote it.

Before I finish, I want to leave you with this short passage about what I took away from losing Dwayne.

I look back not at what has been created with LIVIN but at what that very moment felt like when we lost a beautiful soul, a best mate, a brother and a son. Life lost another great human being to an illness that so few know about unless they actually experience it close-up. Until you lose someone you love to suicide, you do not actually expect it to happen to you.

I know Dwayne didn't want to end his life that morning. He just wanted to end the pain. In the moment when you feel so alone and dark, desperation takes over and you tend to make impulsive decisions based on your current state of mind. Decisions that can change your life forever. The materialistic things in life do not come into play, nor do the things you love, because the pain is so severe it clouds all of that. The pain is so deep you feel exhausted, overwhelmed and you slowly lose breath, suffocating in the thick of the head noise that throws daggers at you while you try to dodge them.

My point here is that no matter how you may be feeling right now, there is always someone out there who will help you. There is always someone out there who feels the exact same way as you and you are never alone. It is perfectly normal not to feel okay. Life is full of ups and downs and no matter how good life gets, it won't stay that way and no matter how bad life seems to go, it doesn't stay that way either. That is the beauty of life. It has a sick sense of humour. You were brought into this world for a reason. A purpose. So go on and live your life and smile because the world is better with you in it. Mental illness doesn't discriminate.

A special thank-you goes out to the LIVIN originals: CH, TC, JC, JD and the entire Lally family.

Above all, remember: it ain't weak to speak.

Thoughts and recommendations
Tim Sharp

Sam's story and the story of LIVIN is another great example of turning dark into light, of making tragedy meaningful and ensuring that while sadly, some lives are lost, they need not be wasted. Sam's story is also a wonderful illustration of friendship, and of how the power of relationships can continue even if one member is no longer present.

I never met Dwayne, but I've heard Sam speak of him a few times now and there's little doubt that he was a force to be reckoned with.

If we focus on the positives in this story then he still is a force to be reckoned with due to the great work being done by Sam and Casey.

How easy would it have been for these two young men to just grieve and then either dwell on their loss and/or try to move on?

How easy would it have been for Dwayne to be just another number; just another statistic?

But thankfully he's not. He's much more than that as a result of what can only be described as a fantastic effort from two blokes doing what they can to ensure that silence didn't win out, that more young men and women didn't believe they were all alone or that they couldn't speak out due to fear. Because as they say over at LIVIN, it ain't weak to speak!

Thanks to Sam and Casey we now have a movement that's gaining increasing momentum and great support from thousands of other young people, including some high profile sportsmen and women, and the hierarchy at the NRL.

And like Batyr, and Joey Williams, this movement and all these voices are so very important. For far too long, far too many have suffered in silence, which just perpetuates the myth that mental illness should not be spoken about.

But it should be spoken about. By doing so, people are far more likely to get help. And when people present for professional support they're far more likely to get better. And surely that's something we all want!

So what can we learn from Sam? Well, to begin with, we can see that mental ill-health is not just about the individual who is suffering or who has suffered. It's also about their friends and family and colleagues and everyone, pretty much, with whom they come into contact.

Overcoming the stigma and problems associated with mental ill-health is also not just up to the individual who's suffering. Just as importantly, there's a role we can all play as mates and siblings and parents and children and members of a caring society.

In addition, we can see that the solution to mental health does not just lie with mental health professionals, or politicians, or those directly affected. Anyone and everyone can play a role as Sam and Casey have shown. If we're going to really get on top of this massive issue then everyone will have to play a role because we're all involved in some way or other.

And finally, LIVIN is showing that loss can lead to learning; that grief can lead to giving; and that something terrible can become something terrific if our response is constructive and positive.

I'm sure you've already thought of a few practical tips you can take from this inspiring story but for me, the key points are:

- Accept the negatives in life but don't dwell on them.
- Acknowledge that not everything can be fixed. Instead focus on what constructive actions you can take.
- Anyone can make the world better, including you!
- Do what you can do, every day, in any way, to help even just one person (even if that person is you).
- Go with your strengths. I know Sam has many ideas for LIVIN but at the moment, they're focusing on what they do well, which is making great fashion and marketing and promoting it well to their target audience. So what are you great at and how can you use that to make a difference?

Playing up for the aged

Jean-Paul Bell and Maggie Haertsch

If there were ever two people who exemplify a life of giving and altruism it would be Jean-Paul and Maggie. Both have devoted their lives to those in need: Jean-Paul as one of the founders of the incredible Clown Doctors and now both of them via their Arts Health Institute. It's often said that in giving we receive; if you have ever wondered whether a life of selflessness could produce health and happiness, then read their story and savour their generosity of spirit, love and kindness.

Jean-Paul:

I am sitting in my small hotel room in Khumjong, a three-day walk from Everest base camp in the Solu Khumbu region of Nepal. We are near the end of a three-month tour visiting eighteens schools established by Edmund Hillary's Himalayan Trust; it is their 50th anniversary and the month of my 60th birthday.

My wife Maggie and I are leading a troupe of performers – I am a mime, and there are two acrobats and a clown – and our tour is being documented by a filmmaker. We thought the adventure would be a fascinating story to tell. We were right and it was later broadcast on ABC. It's the first time the Sherpa people have seen a European circus and clown show. The 50th celebration is happening in the original school that Hillary established high up in the mountains. In fact, the school is known as the school in the clouds.

Our young, fit guide went to the Khumjong school as a child (although some years later I heard that he died from stomach cancer). June Hillary, Sir Edmund's widow, had arrived with some other venerables from 1961; they are old climbers, frail, looking like gnarled tree trunks with their leathery faces and fingers like thick sausages. They fly in by helicopter.

It has been an arduous journey for me, dealing with the altitude, the elements and the performances. Twenty-eight shows – and by this stage, one month of walking. But I feel strong and resolute about what Maggie and I have to do when we return to Australia.

Maggie:
We sat in our kitchen and I asked the question: 'Jean-Paul, what would you like to do for your 60th?' And in his true generous style, he wanted to give something back, to honour his childhood hero Sir Edmond Hillary who he knew was less famous for the significant philanthropy he gave to people in Nepal. In particular, Jean-Paul had always wanted to perform in the schools Hillary built.

Jean-Paul has spent a good part of 45 years touring schools across Australia delivering his comedy in a show and mime workshop called A Mime for all Reasons. We calculated that he would have performed to close to one million children. We have experienced priceless moments when we are out together and he is stopped by a 30- or 40-year-old who sat in his audience as a child, and who thanks him for inspiring them to take up a career in the arts.

So his desire to go back to his love of bringing humour and performing skills to children was not such a surprise, but the difficult journey climbing mountainsides day in and day out in Nepal would prove to be a test. An email to the Himalayan Trust resulted in a phone call from Lady June Hillary herself, calling from New Zealand, offering to help with logistics and scheduling. But we would have to find our own funds. She was excited that the children would benefit from such a tour. So the plan was started and we were on our way.

Jean-Paul:
Six months before the tour I had left the Humour Foundation Clown Doctors after fifteen years. It was a charity I had co-founded with my late friend Dr Peter Spitzer in 1996. I was its original creative director. Clown Doctors was everything to me but I could feel, as often founders can, that it just might be time for me to move on.

My parting with the Humour Foundation happened in the middle of the SMILE Study, a randomised control trial funded by the National Health and Medical Research Council. It was a huge study that provided humour therapy inventions to eighteen aged care facilities and 200 elders matched with a control group. I dressed as an Elder Clown, visiting a number of people who were living with dementia, depression and apathy, and who often felt agitated and isolated.

We made weekly visits over a twelve-week period, which had a wonderful effect on many elders. As I was feeling my way in these delightful interactions using my Clown Doctor skills that were honed visiting small children and adolescents, I realised that I was dealing with people who had led long, full lives and that I was in a real, living, breathing library of experiences, pain, suffering and triumph – all the experiences of life. This was very different from children, of course; there was more material to draw on.

One of the questions I had when visiting my ten selected people at each of the nursing homes was, 'What is happening for everybody else?' Moving from clinical care in hospital to clinical care in nursing homes didn't seem a big jump and that's what concerned me; living your remaining life out in what often felt like a clinical outpatient environment – a bed in a nursing home – didn't seem like a lot of fun.

I discussed this with Maggie, who is a former registered nurse and midwife, and over several conversations we decided that with our combined knowledge of the healthcare industry we would start up another non-profit group promoting the use of the arts in health care.

Our first project came in the shape of Play Up. Towards the end of the SMILE Study I changed my 1950s-style civilian dress with a red nose to more of a service model based on elevator attendants or cinema ushers of the 1940s, an era that the elders in care knew well. Importantly for me, we didn't use the red nose anymore.

Using the key attributes of the fool hidden in a serviceable uniform gave me a front-of-house, at-your-service type of character and really made the aged care facility look like a hotel, particularly if you spent time near the front door. When the SMILE Study came to an end, Maggie approached various aged care facilities that took part and asked them to invest in continuing the humour and creative engagement in care. We were given one to start our new venture.

Over a period of time we got a few more involved. Within the first four months we expanded to 30 aged care facilities. We made a film about how it worked with elderly people in care; The Smile Within followed our experiences during the SMILE Study. This documentary was acquired by ABC. The night the film went to air it rated as one of the highest on the *Compass* program. The media that followed found me on Channel 10's *The Project* talking about our fledgling humour therapy program.

When we kicked off our new dream project, we had heard of a particular person of considerable wealth whom we thought to approach with a proposal to start up the Arts Health Institute. The fortuitous five minutes on *The Project* and the fact that this person saw it while considering our ambitious proposal created a four-year partnership. This was an absolute godsend. Maggie and I and our Board knew we would not be where we are today without this person's financial support! There are angels out there for sure. With the business venture now underwritten we had to work out how to grow the Play Up program.

Maggie:

I had never seen Jean-Paul so flat, lifeless, depressed and unable to communicate; he was feeling worthless, tired and drained. I was deeply concerned for his wellbeing and felt I couldn't reach him. I couldn't break through the pervading malaise that had overtaken his spirit. He was getting progressively worse and it came to a point where he needed to make a decision about his future with the Humour Foundation. He had to give up on his baby, his years of dedicated focus on an organisation he co-founded fifteen years previously, realising that he was no longer in tune with its purpose and direction.

I struggled to know what to do, but having experienced similar symptoms and that inevitable black hole you can fall into, I was determined to do what I could to support him to see his purpose and reframe his sense of worth in another way. Although I could stand by the side of someone who I love so deeply, I couldn't take away the pain and despair. The relief that came when he made the decision to leave showed to him that he could find a way through his grief.

I have a research background and know the challenges of translating research findings so they are adopted in everyday practice, known as knowledge translation or implementation science. Getting the film cameras in to follow Jean-Paul showed the public these intimate interactions, and proved to be an invaluable strategy. On the night of the *Compass* broadcast around 400,000 households came to understand what Jean-Paul was doing, what the researchers were finding out about the work's impact and how it provided hope, joy and laughter to many elderly and their families. It shone a light on the growing invisibility of our aged. It appealed to many people in both aged care and the broader community in a profoundly important way by connecting science with the heart of humanity. This is indeed the power of film.

Jean-Paul's grief lasted for some time after his resignation as both a Director on the Board and Creative Director of the Humour Foundation. After sixteen years of doing his life's work he couldn't simply switch off. It probably took the best part of two years before we stopped hearing about life as a Clown Doctor as his reference point in meetings, workshops and forums.

Once the SMILE Study finished we went to Nepal. The combination of heavy exercise and performing I think was a major contributor to Jean-Paul's improved outlook on life. Far away in the mountains we sat together looking out on an extraordinarily beautiful landscape; rugged up and perched on a rock, we had one of the most important conversations that would shape a new future for us and for health care. The conversation went like this:

Maggie: Now that we are almost ready to go home, what do you want to do next?

Jean-Paul: Well, let's start an organisation that can implement the SMILE Study; we need to see changes for aged care.

Maggie: Okay, but I'm not sure I can work with you in an ongoing way. We are married. I don't want to be married with you to my work. How can we manage that?

Jean-Paul: I think it would be okay; we just need to have time away from it. But it's our combined knowledge that will make this successful.

Maggie: Okay, but if this is to be a truly great organisation it can't be about one program – it needs to address the healthcare system by using the arts in an evidence-based therapeutic way like the SMILE Study. We need to be able to scale great ideas and to influence the entire health sector. What we do needs to bring the arts, in many art forms, together with health professionals to create the change we want to see.

This was an ambitious undertaking and we were prepared to give it a go so we agreed to work together, to form a board and register a company that became the Arts Health Institute (AHI). I claim the name as my brainchild. The model was to be a modern charity, a social enterprise that we needed to operate in a commercial capacity to ensure that our services had value enough that organisations would pay for them. With thousands of charities listed in Australia and the constant need to ask for charitable support, we wanted this model to be self-sustainable, create its own financial stability and run like a business; any profits made would go into research and development on new initiatives. The opportunities ahead were immense. It was to become a fast-growing start-up. On 5 July 2011 the first board meeting was held a week after we arrived home.

Jean-Paul:

How to clone Jean-Paul was the single most repeated comment that came out of the Smile Within documentary and during discussions with aged care service providers. Somewhere in the back of my mind I had a formula that was a template of how I cast, trained and developed performers to work in a hospital environment, so to create a similar model for aged care nursing homes wasn't a big leap. I am also lucky to be connected with many talented performers around Australia who do stand-up comedy, the toughest of places to develop humour. The skill of reading the room was the basis of my performance: love, compassion, empathy and humour creates an instant heart connection when people are in crisis or suffering trauma. About twelve people attended our first casting session. The dream was growing and the humour valets were born!

The valet jacket colour was a maroon and we all wore a fez – in its own unique way it's a type of comic handle and makes people think of Tommy Cooper, magicians and storytellers. Educating our performers about this play-orientated approach turned out to be delightfully fun. They more than got it and some just excelled while others trod carefully and took their time to understand how it worked for them. They just couldn't and shouldn't be a clone of Jean-Paul for Play Up to be successful.

I have always thought that the talents of performing artists are underutilised when you think of the investment they have made in study and training at drama or music school. The arts are about living and sustaining us, and they must be applied to nourish people who are sick, frail or vulnerable. The Arts Health Institute keeps implementing newly discovered and our own creative programs incorporating the talents and skills of a myriad of comics, clowns, musicians, actors, dancers, cabaret artists, street performers and circus performers. We are employing over 70 people in various projects nationwide, making us one of the largest employers of artists in the country – and we are growing.

What pleases me the most is that our artists are often the most talented. The expressions of interest from people who register their desire to join the Institute come from various highly talented individuals who want to give of themselves to sick, frail and aged people. For a performer, it is an opportunity to give their best performance safe in the knowledge that it's not about them!

This new service sector is growing. There is an increasing number of performers employed in arts and health around the world in hospitals, palliative care centres and aged care facilities. You want the best people performing for and inspiring people who are going through difficult and challenging times.

Maggie:
You need guts, sheer bloody-mindedness and ambition to birth an idea. We started with blind faith, drawing on Jean-Paul's years of experience of working in hospitals to cast, train and employ the right kind of artists. We said that cloning Jean-Paul was impossible, but the method can be completely replicated. We worked from a set of principles and developed quality processes

to support the artists and provide them with direction. Jean-Paul and I had trouble keeping up with the demand. We worked hard to support the teams we were developing and to support those incredible aged care providers – those early adopters who believed in the vision, understood the research evidence and made the effort to create the change. Those aged care providers are still with us today as we celebrate our fourth birthday.

Our Play Up program is now in almost 100 aged care facilities and our extraordinary artists are giving joy and humour to of 2000 individuals every week. Further research has demonstrated that the use of antipsychotic and benzodiazepine medications has significantly reduced and we know that there are follow-on effects of decreased falls, agitation and depression. We have also measured a significant improvement in staff morale and happiness at work as well as a decrease in unplanned sick leave. We provide Play Up to some of the most remote aged care facilities with dedicated valets making long road trips on specially designed rural circuits.

The Arts Health Institute now provides many other programs, and works with five universities providing health professional placements and collaborating on research projects, and this continues to grow. We have trained hundreds of aged care workers on how to be more playful at work, which in turn improved productivity as well as directly improving depression and isolation levels of the elders they are caring for.

We work with the most remarkable organisations, artists and individuals. We have come a long way from where we started, and I still pinch myself when I look around our office each day, remembering the time in the mountains of Nepal and the important conversation.

Thoughts and recommendations
Tim Sharp

I first met the inimitable Jean-Paul Bell at Woodford Folk Festival, in the Children's Festival area. He was teaching my son and a number of other young children some wonderful magic and clowning tricks. My son absolutely loved it.

I started up a conversation with this man who I could tell from the first minute was passionate about what he did and cared deeply about the importance of children enjoying fun and play.

Although he was incredibly modest and humble, it didn't take long for a few pennies to drop. I soon realised I was talking to a legend of the Australian performing arts and one of the original founders of the fabulous Clown Doctors. It dawned on me that I was in the presence of a true living legend.

But as is his way, Jean-Paul soon turned the conversation to me and my work and mention of The Happiness Institute piqued his interest. One thing led to another as we both expressed mutual admiration and I'm pleased to say that a friendship was born.

We kept in touch and not long after this initial meeting, Jean-Paul invited me to the inaugural gathering of what went on to become the Arts Health Institute. We collaborated on a few projects and continue to explore ways in which we can help each other help others.

And this final point is what stands out every time I meet and talk to Jean-Paul – his whole life and being and purpose is about helping others.

More recently I've come to know Maggie and although her profile is not quite as prominent as Jean-Paul's, I've learnt that she plays just as integral a role in the AHI. In fact, one of many things I've learnt from this admirable and wonderful couple is the importance and power of team work. Jean-Paul and Maggie work so well together; they complement each other so perfectly, and they do it all so magnanimously.

So what do I take from Maggie and Jean-Paul's story and life work?

I think we can all learn the importance of giving to and serving others. Anyone who's ever met Jean-Paul and Maggie, especially if you've seen or heard them talk about their work, will see the happiness and joy and pride shine from their faces as they illustrate the somewhat clichéd but totally valid truth, in giving we receive.

I think we can also learn the importance of perseverance. As Jean-Paul tells it, it took quite some time for the Clown Doctors to establish credibility, trust and respect, but not for one moment were he and his colleagues deterred or distracted from their belief and purpose.

It's also worth reflecting on the lessons we can learn about walking away and, dare I say it, giving up. Although I wouldn't describe Jean-Paul's departure from the Clown Doctors as giving up or failing in any way, I do believe we all have moments in our lives when we could – or when we need to – let go and move on.

Persistence is so valued in our society, as it should be, but too often too many persist for too long when it may actually be wiser and better to finish up one thing and move on to another.

How else will we ever start something new?

So if you're looking to start something new or redirect your life in some way, what can you take away and implement in your own life? How about trying the following:

- Find something about which you're passionate and go for it with everything you have.

- Find other people who are also passionate about the things you are and surround yourself with complementary strengths and supportive others.

- Don't be afraid to let something go so you can start something else.

- And remember, always, that in serving and helping others we're ultimately helping ourselves. Selflessness and selfishness need not be mutually exclusive but rather, I encourage you to consider how taking care of yourself is vital for taking care of others and also, how doing good for and to others is ultimately doing good for yourself.

The enemy within

Joe Williams

Most normal young men, especially young Indigenous men, don't talk about mental health problems or, in fact, anything that might in any way be indicative of vulnerability or weakness. Thankfully for all of us, Joey Williams is not a normal young man; and for that he's all the stronger! Joe played rugby league for South Sydney, Penrith and Canterbury before switching to professional boxing in 2009. Joe and his story of struggle and everyday victory is admirable for so many reasons, and his inclusion in this collection is something about which I'm very proud.

I was just a young Aboriginal Wiradjuri boy born into a sporting family in Cowra NSW, Australia. It wasn't money and flashy cars – my family did it tough – but we got by. Looking back, the reason we got by was the love and respect we had for each other, and the respect we had within the community.

My family consists of Mum, Dad, a brother and two sisters. My mum, Lee, still to this day holds all the pieces to the puzzle – an extremely strong woman who is the rock in our family. My father, Wilfred, was a gifted sportsman on the rugby league field but also handy with his fists inside the boxing ring –

a hard worker who looked after the family. Michael is my older brother. I idolised him growing up, and everything about him. I would back myself against most people on the rugby league field, but not Mike; he was lengths in front of me in all aspects of rugby league. My younger sisters Jasmine and Aleesha were born one year and four days apart – they are similar in age and in all aspects of their lives. They still struggle to spend a few days apart, which shows how close they really are.

We have always had a close association with our extended family. As you may know, Aboriginal people have a huge extended family, both related and non-related. I remember huge games of touch footy and rounders (like softball), laughs, barbecues and music. Music and sport have gone hand in hand in my life, and have played major roles in me defeating my demons.

As long as I can remember I have always wanted to be a rugby league player. I grew up watching and following the game and the players like it was my religion, emulating players, commentating my own moves in the backyard. But I could never beat my big brother!

We moved to Wagga Wagga in 1993 to follow Dad with his country football contracts – footy paid a significant part of the bills. Mum tells us it was a flip of the coin to either move to Wagga or Dubbo – having spent time later in life in Dubbo, I'm grateful we headed to Wagga.

Wagga was a great place with tremendous opportunities for us kids, and this was the major reason we left Cowra. Not that Cowra was a bad place; there just seemed to be more going for us in Wagga.

Life in Wagga was great. I had a good family life and went to a school that offered lots of sport. I was the first person from the Riverina to captain the NSW PSSA (primary schools) rugby league team. I made heaps of new friends away from sport, too. Wagga was a top move for the family.

My teenage years proved a little more difficult. Like most teenagers, I experimented with alcohol and under-age binge drinking (drugs didn't come until later in life).

I was thrust into a fairly high level of sport at a relatively young age, playing first grade rugby league in the Group 9 competition from the age of fourteen, which was an adult environment and unfortunately had a culture of binge drinking. I believe this was the catalyst for my problems with alcohol later in life.

I moved to Sydney to chase my dream. For some kids it would have been a great opportunity, but for me, it was probably one of the biggest life lessons I could ever learn.

The day I called my mother to say that I had signed a contract with the South Sydney Rabbitohs she cried tears of joy that one day she'd get to see her boy run out in the green and red.

I still remember the day I was due to make my NRL debut. I didn't sleep a wink the night before, and everything I did in preparation for the day of the game turned into a nightmare. I took every wrong turn to get to Shark park and was late to the warm-up. All the players laughed because I was a screaming mess with nerves and was late, to make it even worse.

We lost the game, as we did many that year, but one thing stood out for me that night. My idol, great friend and later mentor Dave Peachey was playing in his 200th NRL game and he said to me, 'Young brother, as my career is nearing its end, yours is just starting – be a leader for all the young Aboriginal kids out there. Work hard and good luck.' The Peach and I are still very close friends. Everything that I do for the community, being a good role model, I learnt from him.

The 2004 season was a great introduction to the top grade. It had its highs and lows. The one thing I could feel was getting the better of me was ego – something I always promised myself I wouldn't let happen. It's tough to keep control of, especially when you're a young kid from the bush, and you have restaurant owners inviting you to eat for free, you don't have to line up in nightclub lines, or pay for drinks. It's fair to say that within twelve months the bright lights got to me.

In 2005, I started the year playing first grade, but was dropped after eight games. The heavy drinking continued and my drug use picked up. I could not go to the pub and have a quiet beer without looking for a bag of cocaine or taking ecstasy tablets or speed. On some occasions I used ice. And often called in sick to training because I was too intoxicated from the previous night or coming down from heavy drug use. I missed a midweek training session because I was out with a heap of school friends from Wagga at an Oasis concert. Another time I was so out of it that I called my reserve grade coach to explain why I was late to training and he replied that it was our day off.

At the beginning of 2006 I joined a church group after saying to myself, 'You can't drink at church.' After three weeks I turned up to church drunk. I then realised I had a drinking problem. The next week I joined Alcoholics Anonymous.

I struggled to stay drink and drug free. My team mates and even my coach knew little about alcoholism. In 2007 I asked my coach if I could be excused from a Christmas function as I felt uncomfortable with the alcohol and as it was on a cruise it was hard to escape the temptations. He replied, 'It's okay. Just have a few quiet drinks and don't go over the top.'

I was clean and sober for over a year, but I still battled with my alcohol and drug addictions. During this time I developed depression. I then turned to prescription drugs as these were easily accessed by lying to doctors to get scripts or from other injured players, and they were not detected by drug testers. I would go home after training and get completely out of it by taking extreme amounts of prescription sleeping pills, painkillers, antipsychotic pills – you name it I had a crack at it! Some days my kids would be jumping all over me, wanting to play with me and I was too high to even register they were there. Some days I would be so low that I would take as many pills as I could to test my tolerance, and think about not waking up.

This carried on until I decided to go cold turkey with prescription drugs also. This detox was the worst experience of my life: hot and cold sweats, not being able to sleep, even hallucinations. I was so paranoid that I was afraid to leave my bedroom and thought at times that the world was set against me.

In early 2010 I went through a destructive marriage breakdown. I didn't see or speak with my two eldest children,

Brodi and Phoenix, for fifteen months. This sent my depression even lower – to the point where I could not physically get out of bed some days.

In 2011 I was diagnosed with bipolar disorder and continue to be medicated for both bipolar and depression. I stopped taking my meds for six months, which culminated in an unsuccessful suicide attempt midway through 2012.

I still remember that day as if it were yesterday: the thoughts, the smells, even what I was wearing. I was going through a particularly tough time due to another relationship breakdown. I was living in Dubbo, coaching the local Dubbo CYMS football team. Things were pretty decent on the field; we were sitting near the top of the ladder and the season was progressing okay. Things off the field weren't.

While battling with the demons of depression in my own mind, I was also battling with my partner at the time. The disagreements mostly came about because of my parenting skills and/or lack of help with our newborn, Rome Joseph. Looking back I wasn't the best, but I guess I was just too stubborn to see it at the time.

After hearing you're worthless, good for nothing, a terrible father by not just one, but two different mothers of your kids, chances are you start to believe it. This particular day I was extremely vulnerable and down due to my depression as well, and this is when I first had suicidal thoughts. The thoughts and voices in my head were so overpowering I saw it as my only option. As I lay curled up on my shower floor, crying my eyes out, I began to think that this was the only answer to make it all go away. I also began to believe my three children, Brodi, Phoenix and Rome, would be better off without me in their lives.

I was convinced. I got out of the shower and sat down to write letters to each of my kids. I told them how much I loved them, how I was sorry I couldn't be there for them growing up and that I would be their angel in the sky they could talk to every night when they needed a yarn. I finished with, 'You will never walk alone – just look up (one of the tattoos I had inked on my arm). Love you always, Dad xx.'

I swallowed as many sleeping pills and antipsychotic pills as I could find in my house, lay on my bed, said a prayer thanking God for the life I had lived, asked Him to please take care of the kids, and slowly began to drift off, hoping that I would never wake up.

The next morning, when I opened my eyes, I didn't know whether to be happy I'd woken up or disappointed that I wasn't dead. Either way, I learnt pretty fast that my living had happened for a reason and I consciously made the decision to not let my second chance at life disappear from my grasp.

A week later I admitted myself to Dubbo Hospital where I spent three nights in the mental health ward. This was the most vulnerable I have ever felt. It was an extremely scary time.

Our deepest fear
Is not that we are inadequate
Our deepest fear is that
We are powerful beyond measure.
It is our light, not our darkness

That most frightens us.
We ask ourselves,
Who am I to be brilliant, gorgeous
Talented and fabulous?
Actually, who are we not to be?

When I first heard this quote by Marianne Williamson in the movie *Coach Carter* I didn't quite understand it. Now, a few years on and having experienced my fair share of disappointments and setbacks, I can relate to it more. I was born and blessed, thanks to my parents, with fantastic athletic ability. As a kid, any sport I played, I excelled at. As I grew up, especially when it came to sport, things all came a little too easily. There was a time when I was injured with a broken thumb and didn't play the NSWCCC Rugby League trials, yet all I had to do was submit a letter stating I was injured and I was still the first kid picked.

One thing that haunted me, even from a young age, was my inner fear. What if I tried my absolute best and it wasn't good enough? My deepest fear was that my best would be inadequate. My deepest fear was that if I tried my absolute best, and fell short, I would be lost and emotionally hurt. I wouldn't know how to get the best out of myself.

Throughout my entire NRL career, I had the same attitude. I just did enough to get by, thinking I was fooling everyone – everyone but myself. Still to this day I wish I'd had the same attitude towards my training and preparation as I do now with my boxing, but I guess that was a very valuable lesson I had to learn for later in my journey.

I had glimpses of me beating this inner fear. There would be times, in the final moments of a game, when we needed a big play to get us over the line, to win the game. Like the time we won the Jersey Flegg Grand Final while playing for the Sydney Roosters. It was a grand final; I had to stand up. When I had to I would. We came from behind and the scores were tied with about two minutes left on the clock. I demanded the ball 35 metres out from the opposition line and hit the sweetest field goal I have ever kicked in my career – we won the game by one point.

Even in my many relationships away from the football field, I would never give myself entirely to the woman I loved. Again because of the fear of getting hurt. This was not fair on the partner I was involved with at the time as they would give me their complete loyalty and trust but I couldn't. I still have problems with trust; this is why I let very few people inside my inner circle. I have been burnt by those I'd deemed close to me in the past and this is something I'm still extremely conscious of.

Back to my deepest fear. My father told me a story not long after I was released from the Dubbo mental health ward: the story of the little boy inside us all. This story resonated with me and to this day I use it in situations. This story helped me conquer my inner fears.

Sitting on the front step at my Dubbo home, Dad said to me, 'I want to tell you about the story of the little boy. There is a little boy (or girl) who lives in us all. He is guided by you, or he controls you. Every now and then, that little boy encounters a situation that frightens him, to the point where he wants to go deep inside you and hide, and not show his face. In each situation, he is faced with a door; he can either walk through the door, or go back and hide. You are with this little boy, you come to the door, what do you do?'

I quickly replied, 'Kick the door down so he can walk through.'

My father's reply implanted the seed in my mind that helped to conquer my inner fears.

The advice was about guidance: 'Take that little boy by the hand and say to him, "I'm here with you, let's do this together." Lead that little boy; be his guiding light, together as one. You and he together can conquer any obstacle you face.'

This advice I carry with me every single day. I am like most people in the world – I have fears, insecurities. But I know that I have to guide this little boy inside – who often pops up; during physical confrontations, in the ring, while I'm doing the hard yards in the gym, or facing the temptations of everyday life – and not let him control me.

My boxing career has also given me the strength to face my inner battles – every single day. Boxing has helped train not only my physical fitness but my deep inner mentality and ability to confront fear.

Every single time I step inside that gym, I am faced by situations that scare that little boy deep inside. When things get hard physically in training, it tests me mentally. When these situations arise, you can either run or hide, or you can guide that little boy through the tough situations. Once upon a time, I was not able to stand strong in tough situations – I would run and hide. Now, when I search deep inside myself, I like the person I find – that person is a strong warrior, happy to guide that little boy through and gratefully out the other side.

As a boxer I have been lucky enough to win twelve of my sixteen professional fights, with only three losses and one draw. I have been fortunate to win the WBF World title twice and also the WBC Asia Continental title. Not bad for a young kid from the bush who never had experience as an amateur boxer before turning professional. The day I decided to be a boxer, I knew I wouldn't be the greatest ever boxer, but as long as I continue to learn about the sport, live a clean, healthy lifestyle and learn more about myself every single day – I am content with how it is progressing.

Another reason I love my boxing is that there is something freeing about walking into a gym. A weight is lifted from my shoulders, my demons and mental health battles diminish, and for that short period I spend inside those four walls my mind is at peace.

I was always going to return to country life. I'd spent the longest period in my life living in Sydney, but still I couldn't warm to the place. The noise, the traffic and overall business of the big smoke was enough to convince me that I will always be a bush boy.

I am lucky that I've had a lot of my life portrayed in a positive light; that I am someone who my community see as a role model. This is something I have great pride in every day. A role model, to me, isn't someone who sets a good example from 9 am to 5pm in his job – I live my life as a role model. I try my best to be the mirror image I would like to see, of what I believe a role model looks like.

A big part of being a positive role model is not letting myself interact with negative influences. There is a difference between someone who genuinely wants to be helped and people who only associate with you when it suits them, or who just want to dump their baggage on you. This is something I have learnt the hard way many times in my short life.

I put a lot of my kind nature down to the way I was raised by my parents. As a family we didn't have a great deal, but we had always been taught to be grateful for what we had because someone, somewhere, is always doing it that little bit harder.

For as long as I can remember, I had always felt bad for having certain things that were better, more expensive, than other people's. Material things mean nothing to me. I don't need the flash houses, cars, boats – as long as I have a roof over my head, clothes on my back and food in my stomach – nothing else matters. To me, as long as you have good health, a caring heart and compassion for others, the rest does not matter. Take all the material possessions away, and it's your soul that matters. A huge part of who I am is the compassion I have for everyone I come into contact with.

Since returning home to Wagga I have been involved with multiple fundraising efforts, raising money for those in need. I am an ambassador for numerous trusts and charities. The Amie

St Clair Melanoma Trust is one that I hold dear to my heart. I grew up next door to the St Clair family during the late nineties. Amie was the only daughter of Pete and Annette St Clair, who also had a son, Tim. Amie tragically lost her life to melanoma a day after her 21st birthday. She was a loving, caring, outgoing girl who lived life to the fullest, and she was tragically taken away from a great family far too young. I am the ambassador for the St Clair foundation and jump at any opportunity to raise funds and raise awareness around melanoma/skin cancer.

Another fundraising opportunity I jumped at was Wagga Wagga Takes Two, a singing competition that pairs up local Wagga singers with people of note within the community. I have grown up with music and love the feeling of being on stage in front of a band. Each individual identity chooses a local charity to support and the overall winner is awarded to the couple who raises the most amount of money for their charity.

The charity I chose was the 2013 Cancer Council's Wagga Relay for Life. It's another charity close to my heart as I have lost many family and friends to cancer. Each contestant was to organise a fundraiser for their local charity. I decided to do something outside the square. I run my own boxing and cardio fitness gym so I decided to host a 24-hour charity treadmill run as a community event: two treadmills, one runner, with at least one treadmill running the entire 24 hours.

At first people thought that I would be running for the entire 24 hours … definitely not. The idea was to break the 24 hours down into fifteen-minute timeslots for different people.

I put the call out for people to throw up their hand to participate. The response was great and showed true community spirit. I had volunteers ranging from family and friends, ladies aged 60-plus, students from the school I work at, to local sporting identities, and parents with their kids. The community involvement was typical of Wagga: everyone jumped behind this local charity event to raise funds.

The Cancer Council staff put on a barbecue, tea and coffee, and my local sponsors all donated time and gear to use, such as treadmills, clothing apparel and water.

Three, two, one … the treadmill started and I was first cab off the rank to get the charity run underway. People had the choice to donate online, come in and donate cash or purchase raffle tickets. There was also a 24-hour live auction for an Aboriginal hand painted AFL Sydney Swans jersey signed by Australian of the Year Adam Goodes. It was definitely an experience I won't forget.

I had to stay at the gym the whole time. Whether I was awake or not, I had to stay to make sure it all ran smoothly. For the first twelve hours I was awake, I was pretty much flying on adrenaline. All the runners turned up on time and people off the street were dropping into the gym to cheer on friends and support the event by donating.

We had all types of people drop in, from local larrikins from the local drinking hole to police officers. Some girls even randomly popped in to touch up their make-up while they waited for a couple of the local footy studs to hit the tready. Some girls paid extra money to see the boys run with no shirt on – all for charity they said. We made it through the night with no major hiccups, and as the afternoon approached we were getting down to the final legs. In fitting style, I chose to start and finish the event. I ended up doing seven hours in total on the treadmill. As I finished the final hour, thankfully I had my family there to count me down.

Three, two, one … we were finished. Twenty-four hours, two treadmills, one continuous runner. We made over $10,000 from the raffles, auction and donations, which was an awesome achievement.

Since 2013 and my return to my home town, I have been involved in numerous campaigns helping to raise a combined total of about $200,000 for charities both local and national. This is something I am extremely proud of. I am passionate about providing those in a less fortunate position with an opportunity to better the situation they are faced with. Again, I attribute this to the way I was raised.

In October 2014, a short film titled *The Enemy Within* was released. It's the story about my depression and how it drove me to the brink of suicide. The film is beautifully scripted by my good friend Simone Dowding, in consultation with selected psychologists.

Although the vision of *The Enemy Within* was to help others come through the other side like I have done, I reacted to it emotionally. Having my past struggles brought up again really hit home as to how real it was and how very lucky I am to still be alive.

The adverse reaction personally took a heavy toll – my poker face was revealed. I could no longer pretend everything was okay. I had to front up to my demons, look them dead in the eye and push through.

The carefully worded script, however, was the remedy that helped me out of the really dark times. The hidden messages: if you can't walk then crawl, but whatever you do, you have to keep moving forward; and how every great person in life had to start somewhere.

It is these messages I carry close to me every single day. It is these messages that I use to spread my messages of inspiration. It is these messages that I use as hope to those who have been in a similar position, in the depths of darkness in the grip of the dreaded depression – my enemy within.

Having gained a great deal of exposure from the short film, I decided I wanted to help people on a more frequent basis. With help from a few contacts, it was time to take The Enemy Within Project on the road, to help in schools, youth centres and juvenile justice centres, and also to help adults – pretty much anyone and anybody who wanted to seek inspiration from my story. I have even been invited to speak with the NRL Indigenous All Stars, and at corporate events and conferences.

While I was on the road meeting people, I began to realise that depression and mental health were becoming huge issues in our rural communities. The more people I spoke to, the more I became aware of a common theme: when we are in a time of need we all feel so alone.

Through my Facebook page The Enemy Within: Depression Awareness and Motivational Wellbeing, I have connected with many people in need of advice or just the odd word of hope to try to pull them away from the dark shadows. I'm very proud that people feel confident enough to talk to me and trust me to be able to guide them out of their troubled times; it's truly humbling.

I have made contact with and assisted numerous people through their difficult times. I always offer my help to anyone who needs it; again, because I was raised well and I am compassionate towards everyone. A great piece of advice I got was, 'Always treat people well, cos everyone is fighting their own battle we know nothing about.'

During the past six months my spiritual journey has had a massive boost. I lived in Sydney for a big chunk of my life, and I found it hard to connect to my Aboriginality. I believe this has been a huge part of my returning home to Wagga – connecting with Mother Earth on my home Wiradjuri country. The older I get, the closer I feel to the spiritual side of my culture; the learning and sharing of stories, and continually paying my respects to Mother Earth. This journey is a progressive one and probably will end up being the most significant in my life. When I work with children in schools, I get the chance to share what knowledge I have with both Indigenous and non-Indigenous kids every single day. The most important people I get to share this knowledge with are my children, so they can carry our culture into the future.

I also talk to the broader community, not only about Indigenous culture but about being kind, respectful and humble in their journey. I encourage people to be the best possible version of themselves whatever that may be. If you are a professional athlete, a politician or a garbage collector, be the absolute best you can be at your job and do what makes you happy.

Every day I thank my spirit, my higher powers, that I have a beautiful fiancée Courtney and four wonderfully talented, happy and humble children – Brodi (ten), Phoenix (nine) Rome (four) and Ari (ten months).

At 32, I'm living and loving life, and continuing to chase my dreams every single day.

I always tell every audience I speak with, in closing, that everybody has the ability to dream – it is up to you how hard you chase those dreams.

Thoughts and recommendations
Tim Sharp

I knew Joe Williams before I knew Joe Williams. That is, being a keen rugby league fan I'd been aware of Joe's playing career as he came into first grade and put in impressive performances for several teams. More recently, however, I saw an article about some of Joe's work and was immediately intrigued. Here was a young Indigenous man, an ex-footy player, openly talking about his struggles with depression, suicidal thoughts, drugs and alcohol.

Although these issues are prevalent in young males, it's not common for this group of people to openly or publicly talk about such problems. So when I read about Joe talking about these things and doing what he could to help others, I was impressed by his courage and honesty, and his desire to make a positive contribution.

I then reached out to Joe, made contact online and had several phone conversations as well as multiple email communications. I'm pleased to say that he's just as (if not more) impressive in real life!

Joe has a remarkable combination of strength and humility. Having read his story, you'll already know that since retiring from football he has, over recent years, taken up a career in boxing and along the way he's won several titles. So he clearly has physical strength, but I'm actually referring to psychological strength – strength to be vulnerable and resilient and fallible and better. He makes no bones about the mistakes he's made and he's done his best, and is still doing his best, to remedy them. He's constantly trying to be a better person and is increasingly dedicating his time and energies to helping others to be better as well.

So what can we learn from Joe? What can you take away and implement in your own life?

- Don't be afraid to be afraid; fear is a normal part of life and the overcoming of it creates strength and confidence.
- It's okay to admit to mistakes, but it's also important to learn from those mistakes and make up for them where possible.
- It's okay not to be perfect, but it's also important to strive to be better.
- Coping with depression is an ongoing process. Day by day, and step by step Joe shows us that although life can be challenging at times, it can also be manageable.
- One of the ways Joe shows us that life can be better managed is by surrounding yourself with supportive and loving people.

None of us can be our best on our own; we all need help and support. So find those people who can help you and spend as much time with them as possible!

- Joe's fantastic illustration of the great concept that suggests in giving we receive; by helping others, Joe is helping himself.
- Being vulnerable is not the same as being weak. As one of our other contributors says, 'it ain't weak to speak'! Joe (and Seb and Sam and others) teach us that speaking out helps everyone involved so find an appropriate person, or several people, or a group or forum or community in which you'd be comfortable to talk about those issues that cause you distress.
- And finally, whenever you feel overwhelmed, break your problems down into smaller, more manageable chunks. This always helps me and it's something that Joe talks a lot about. Happiness and success comes one step and one day at a time. Sometimes, that's all we need to do – just take that one step. What's your next step?

Surviving to thriving

Justine Curtis

Some people fall into and stay stuck in the daily grind of a job, doing what's expected, and living lives of quiet (or not so quiet) desperation! Justine is not one of these people. Thankfully so because as a result of leaving the corporate sector and starting up Inspired Adventures in 2004, thousands upon thousands of people have benefitted from the $20 million the company has raised. And just as importantly, Justine's story provides inspiration for anyone and everyone who'd like 'something better'.

What lead me to where I am today? Mine is the same old story really. I was trapped in the cold clutches of the corporate world where life was simply the repetition of a meaningless, unfulfilling cycle of events.

After graduating university in 1993 with a historical studies degree, I secured a job with a London publishing house in media sales. It wasn't exactly the direction I sought to take, so after three years I left to see the world. I craved the physical, cultural and spiritual manifestations of the countries I had learnt so much about during my time at university.

Of particular interest to me was Vietnam, a country and its people so terribly ravaged by war, yet still displaying a resilient spirit and steely resolve to rise and thrive. I booked a group tour and we took in the sights and sounds of this fascinating country, journeying from Hanoi in the north to Ho Chi Minh in the south. The experience of getting under the skin of a country was thrilling: homestays, cycle adventures, overnight trains and many other enthralling ventures.

After Vietnam, I was tempted by Thailand and the thrill of backpacking where every day was a new adventure. I was entranced by Indonesia, in awe of the archipelago, and eventually arrived in Australia full of admiration for this weird and wonderful world we live in.

Sadly it was there the wonder – the flame that drove my thirst for adventure and knowledge – was extinguished. I accepted a position with a direct-marketing company working on sales and marketing with IT clients and once again settled in to a life defined and diminished by routine. I woke up each morning, collected my coffee from the same old cafe and sat down at my desk. For three and a half hours I made cold calls until my lunchtime reprieve. Then it was back to my desk with the phone at my ear until five when I trudged back home with little sense of any achievement.

It was the same old mundane Monday to Friday cycle. I would get through the working week, but I'd constantly crave the respite of the weekend. Once Sunday night came around, I knew I'd have to get up the next morning and face it all again – a thought I could hardly bear.

That's not to say I wasn't good at my job. I have always

had a knack for sales and marketing. I was fifteen when I got my first job working in a call centre in England. I sat at a tiny desk with the phone book working through it alphabetically, calling each name and offering them a deal they simply couldn't refuse. Okay, to be honest, it was the offer of a free quote on a kitchen refurbishment. Yet with an enthusiasm I did not share for the product I was selling, I converted numerous cold calls into hot leads and became one of the highest paid salespeople in the company.

However, just because you're good at something doesn't necessarily mean you enjoy it. With weeks turning into months and eventually years, I went on – the days renewing and repeating, but never changing. My resolve was quickly waning. I wanted to be doing work that was fulfilling, something I was passionate about and something that would give me enjoyment. I didn't believe that life was just about earning a living and going through the paces. I clung onto the belief that living was so much more than that.

It was during another ordinary day that I had an epiphany. I would once again pack my bags, leave the city behind and explore the world. There was just so much more I wanted to see and do. I think this is something many people wish they could do, but are often too afraid to make the change and take a chance on themselves. It's scary to leave behind what you know and what society deems the normal way of living. But from fear often comes the greatest change – and the greatest reward. More people need to have faith in themselves and know that if they want to take their life path in a different direction, they absolutely can.

What truly pushed me to take a chance was the fact that I had an undeniable desire to reconnect with my spiritual self. I would often sit at my desk and wonder what was happening in the world. I wanted to know how others who worked so hard seemed to effortlessly achieve that balance between their passions and getting paid that had so far eluded me. I had to know how they discovered the difference between simply living life and being alive. But this time it was different. It wasn't simply the desire to escape the daily grind. It was an unwavering, ceaseless call to action that I could no longer ignore.

I had always been intrigued by India, so after resigning in 2000 I made my way through Mexico, Morocco and Africa and eventually to India, not knowing it would be in this incredible country that my life's path would be forever changed.

It was on a train between Delhi and Dharamsala, where I was planning to volunteer at a local school, that I first picked up *Fire Under the Snow* by Palden Gyatso. This inspirational story is the testimony of a Tibetan political prisoner held captive by Chinese forces in Tibet. One man's journey of suffering and endurance, from surviving to thriving, it was a book I simply could not put down.

Palden Gyatso was born in 1933 in a small Tibetan village. At age eighteen he became an ordained Buddhist monk and served his faith at Tibet's renowned Drepung Monastery.

During the Lhasa uprising against the Chinese occupation of Tibet in 1959, nine years after the initial invasion, Palden was arrested for protesting and sentenced to 33 years imprisonment. He was just 28 years old.

Throughout his imprisonment, Palden endured severe physical and emotional torture, often at the hands of fellow inmates who were forced to perform the beatings and denounce the Buddhist faith. For extended periods of time, his hands and feet were cuffed. He was exposed to various forms of indoctrination, interrogation and thought reform, and forced to watch brutal executions.

Despite this extreme treatment, Palden resisted the Chinese repression. He remained committed to his faith and became an inspiration to his fellow inmates.

In 1992, Palden was released from Drapchi Prison. Knowing he had to share his knowledge and experience of the Chinese treatment of Tibetans with the world, he escaped to Dharamsala in northern India soon after his release. On his perilous journey over the Himalayas, Palden carried with him instruments of torture like the ones used on him as proof of the inhumane atrocities committed against Tibetan prisoners.

Since resettling in Dharamsala, Palden has spoken extensively about his experiences and the treatment of Tibetans by the Chinese. To date, he has spent more years behind bars than any other surviving Tibetan that has reached the West.

So one day while I was still travelling, I joined a local Tibetan for a cup of tea. I told him about the book I had read and how it had affected me. My companion suddenly turned to me and excitedly said, 'I know him. He lives around the corner. I'll take you to him.'

I was absolutely beside myself.

He led me to a small apartment and inside was a tiny man who radiated the most amazing aura of hope and positivity. I have met the Dalai Lama and the feeling of meeting Palden was very similar.

I spoke with him for a few hours, drinking tea and eating biscuits. It was like any normal afternoon tea with a friend, but at the same time it was so much more. Just being in the same room as Palden was almost magical; the energy in the air was palpable. Here was a man so strong, and so resilient; he had gone through something no human should ever have to. The whole experience was quite surreal.

His nephew was there with us, acting as a translator. Yet without even speaking the same language as Palden, I could feel his determined spirit and resilient nature.

Perhaps, however, what I will remember most about meeting Palden was when we said goodbye. Life is different in developing countries and, after my sabbatical, I was intimidated about returning to my commercial, fast-paced life in Australia. So I asked Palden how I could continue to embrace this feeling of purpose in the Western world.

With tears streaming down his face, he grabbed my head between his hands and touched his forehead to mine. He said, 'Do dharma. Do good work. Be it.'

So I did.

In October 2001 I returned to Australia with a new purpose. I secured a position in the fundraising industry and oversaw the creation of Australia's largest face-to-face fundraising agency. Applying my knowledge and experience of big business marketing, in just three years I grew the business to over 250 employees and led my team in raising $25 million for not-for-profit organisations.

I learnt a lot during this time, from how to run a company and manage staff to financial business acumen and how to grow a business organically. I was so interested in business management that I enrolled in a management training course. It was from part of an assessment for the course that I came up with the idea of raising $30,000 to climb Mount Kilimanjaro and fund the development of a water pump for an AIDS orphanage in Zimbabwe. In just three months.

When the idea hit me, I tried to dismiss it. When travelling through Tanzania I'd had the opportunity to climb Kilimanjaro but said no. I believed I couldn't do it, that it required months, even years, of training and preparation.

However, despite trying to fight it – and going against every one of my carefully established fibres to avoid risks – the feeling that this was something I had to do was overwhelming.

I had never fundraised personally before. Sure, I could motivate a team to coach others to their fundraising targets, but I had no idea where to start when it came to fundraising. There was also the physical aspect. I've always enjoyed yoga and Pilates but to me, running and gym classes are akin to extreme sports. Despite this, every morning from then on I walked with telephone books in my backpack and I even braved step classes.

Without realising it, I had made a complete physical and psychological commitment to my cause. I was amazed at the generosity and support people showed both financially and emotionally, and this only drove my dedication to achieving my goal.

Twelve weeks later I was standing at the summit of the world's highest freestanding mountain and realised that my idea could be used as a tool to build the profitability of charities. Coming to this realisation while gazing out on the East African plains at sunrise was an incredibly powerful feeling. It was in that moment that I knew I wanted to share this feeling with the rest of the world. It was an undeniable realisation that I must continue on this journey, fulfil my commitment to changing myself and helping the world around me.

On my return to Sydney I resigned from my position with the fundraising agency and turned my idea into a business model for what would become Inspired Adventures.

With my business model established, albeit in my own head, I walked into the office of the Australia Tibet Council (ATC) and boldly proclaimed that I was going to create a successful fundraising event for them. Luckily for me, they believed in me and gave me the permission to go ahead.

Working out of my living room I created the itinerary and coordinated the travel arrangements. ATC then sent an email to their database and in next to no time we had twenty community fundraisers signed up for the adventure of a lifetime. Ranging in age from 15 to 69, from all across the country, together they raised over $55,000.

Soon I was travelling back to India on the first Inspired Adventure, the Trek for Tibet, to experience the colour, culture and chaos of Dharamsala – the place where it all began.

As we traversed the northern Indian Himalayas together we forged lifelong friendships through our shared passion to make a difference. It was an experience that would stay with us forever. It was especially amazing to witness the transformation of the 15-year-old – who was travelling through India with his 69-year-old grandmother and eighteen strangers. At first he was a very shy and reserved teenager. However, by the end of the adventure he was dancing around the campfire singing his heart out with the rest of the group.

In 2014 the Australia Tibet Council returned to Dharamsala on a ten-year anniversary adventure. On this reunion adventure the team were privileged to meet the Dalai Lama. It was another incredible sign that the path we are on together leads to great things.

Soon after the Trek for Tibet I signed up more charity partners and, in 2006, I coordinated four Inspired Adventures, raising over $200,000 for Australian charities.

It was starting to feel like my life's purpose was materialising.

I hired my first staff member in 2007, by which point I had already organised fifteen adventures. We moved into an office in the centre of Sydney and soon became a team of three.

In 2008 I received the wonderful news that I was going to become a mother and gave birth to my beautiful girl Indigo later that year.

Naturally, this did of course have an impact on the business growth of Inspired Adventures. However, as many women do, I had to keep going. Just one day after Indigo was born I was on the phone to clients.

It certainly wasn't easy, but for the first year of her life I managed to balance being a new mum with being the founder of a small but steadily growing business. When Indigo slept I worked, strangely being more productive in those little pockets of time. When she was awake, I dedicated my time to bonding with my daughter and giving her the love and attention every child deserves.

Becoming a mother is life-changing in so many ways. There are the obvious changes: the new person that relies on you wholly for survival, the sleepless nights, the agonising over whether you are doing enough, *giving* enough. There are also the subtle changes that only become apparent on reflection. For me, it was a total shift in perspective. My passion for making a difference began to centre on women and girls and their struggles. Poor maternal health, lack of educational opportunities and cruel persecution in many countries resonated with me and affected me more than ever.

Sadly, when Indigo was just a year and a half old, my husband and I decided to separate. Almost overnight I was thrust into the extremely challenging role of single motherhood. Enduring the dissolution of a marriage is difficult enough. Doing so when a child is involved is heart-wrenching. With my family in the United Kingdom, I felt I had nowhere to turn and no-one to rely on. It was then I realised that when you're in the middle of hell, you must keep going. You must keep 'doing good'.

For the next two years I focused on being the best mother I could and devoted the rest of my time to building my business. I learnt how to dig deeper even when it felt like I had nothing left to give. I learnt how to be resourceful. Failure was no longer an option.

I believe during this time it was Indigo that kept me going. She forced me to remain present and mindful. She helped me to appreciate the little things, the little wins. As any mother would know, there is no time that your child doesn't need you. Even when I was working, I was doing it for my daughter.

Starting your own business requires tenacity, dedication and a lot of hard work. When things don't go as planned, your only recourse is to work it out. I worked hard and eventually my little business for good started to make a huge impact.

I've held many senior and executive positions, but none have been more fulfilling than leading and growing my own business for good.

People often talk about work/life balance, and are constantly striving to achieve it. But for me, there is no work/life balance because to be honest, my work is my life. I'm not suggesting that work is all I ever do, but my work and my life seamlessly flow together. Working never feels like work because it's my passion and what I love to do.

From my humble beginnings working out of my living room and creating a business model on the back of an envelope, in just ten years I have led my team in raising $18 million for Australian and international charities. Since then we have continued to raise significant funds and are on track to double our previous achievements in just two years.

I now offer a way for people to facilitate their journey from surviving to thriving. I see myself in our community fundraisers – people eager to make a difference and searching for their way to contribute to a better world.

This wasn't a dream of mine since childhood. My journey from surviving to thriving was a series of events that, nurtured by experience, led me to realise my purpose.

We now work with many incredible charities in Australia and New Zealand including Breast Cancer Network Australia, Unicef Australia, Open Heart International, Cure Brain Cancer Foundation, the Black Dog Institute, Australia for UNHCR and so many more.

We have the honour of meeting the incredible supporters of our charity partners, and through the desire to reach a common goal, we work together to achieve amazing things. We have seen women who are terminally ill with breast cancer cycle over 350 kilometres through Southeast Asia from Vietnam to Cambodia. We have witnessed the dedication of a young blind man who summitted Mount Kilimanjaro after personally raising $35,000 for Guide Dogs NSW. I have watched the relationship between a mother and daughter transform with every step taken along the Inca Trail to Machu Picchu in Peru, and seen how through the power of philanthropy and travel, a team of school students can raise over $100,000. The list goes on and on.

With every year, we are growing exponentially and every day ordinary people are achieving extraordinary things thanks to Inspired Adventures. You may be surprised by how many people want to achieve incredible things but don't know where to begin or how to do it. At Inspired Adventures, we give everyday people the knowledge and the power to fulfil their extraordinary desires, all while helping others in need.

In 2014, our tenth year of operation and auspiciously the same year we reached our $10 million raised milestone, I was nominated for the Telstra Business Women's Award for Business Owner NSW and also Business Innovation. I was told it was one of the rare times that one person had been nominated in two categories.

As part of the nomination process, I was forced to reflect on what I had achieved both personally and professionally. When you're knee-deep in the daily operations of your business, there is simply no time to pat yourself on the back. Your appreciation is reserved for those who work tirelessly to help you achieve your goal. It is only when you are forced to review your career that you begin to appreciate the magnitude of what one person can do with a clear purpose and an unwavering passion.

To my great surprise, I won the Business Owner NSW category. As I prepared to give my acceptance speech, I was entirely humbled that I could compete with the calibre of exceptional women standing before me, all leaders and innovators in their respective fields.

Also sitting in the crowd that night was my amazing partner, Angus, who later that month became my fiancé. Finally finding love like I never imagined was possible, Angus has become a wonderful stepfather to Indigo and has given me a second chance at building a happy and fulfilling family life. As a testament to the bonds formed as part of an Inspired Adventure, four members of the original ATC Trek for Tibet team attended our wedding.

Just a couple of months later, I won the Gold Stevie Award for Women in Business for Entrepreneur of the Year in Asia, Australia or New Zealand – a world recognised top honour for women in business. And in 2015, Inspired Adventures won a Bronze Stevie Award for Corporate Social Responsibility Program of the Year.

Humbled by the influx of accolades, I began to focus on how I could use my experiences to inspire other women to succeed in business and understand the importance of corporate social responsibility.

For many years I have benefitted from the sound and honest advice of my business mentor. She donates her time to me for free and in turn encourages me to consider doing the same for others. I have long believed that with courage and tenacity, there's no limit to the number of women who can become successful, socially minded business women – and I am certain that the world would be a better place if more women took on positive leadership roles.

Mentoring serves as much to support someone else as it helps you to refocus your vision and objectives. It is a fulfilling experience to be involved in the growth stages of a business and is a constant reminder of the passion that first drove me to set out on my own.

Running my business has been an inspired adventure of its own, and every day I learn and grow through my experiences. I now have the confidence in myself, and my business, to lead and inspire other women to create their own businesses for good and be captains of their industry.

Meeting monthly with my two mentees is a valuable experience. Neither operates in the same industry as me – one is an ethical jeweller, the other a yogi establishing an online service – however, we find that the fundamentals of building a successful business are the same regardless of your offering. It is finding the balance between doing and being, understanding your objective and living it.

This is of the utmost importance in my workplace. I lead an incredible team of twenty women (and one wonderful man!) who help me grow my business every single day. Most of them are young, with many fresh out of university or still studying. I am thrilled that these capable, strong and intelligent women have chosen Inspired Adventures to kickstart their careers.

Working with them is an incredible opportunity to see through their optimistic eyes. Together we achieve amazing things and it is a pleasure to watch them develop the confidence, skills and leadership qualities that in the future will mean the difference between a good world and a great world. These women will truly make the future a better and brighter place.

Remember: thriving is not a personal mission. You must learn how to accept help and know when to say no. You have to clearly define your goals and forge the path to achievement. When your passion is pure and pursued out of genuine interest, it becomes organic, natural and ultimately fulfilling. Upon reaching your goal, you must reach your hand back and encourage others to follow in your footsteps. What you'll discover is that with integrity and passion, you can inspire not just one person but a community, a country, even the entire world.

I want to continue to grow my business and establish a sustainable travel agency in the future. I want to become the leading responsible, ethical travel agent in Australia, offering incredible experiences around the world.

Your dreams don't belong in your head. Your dreams need to be realised and set free. If you want to go from surviving to thriving, give it all you've got. When it feels like you've got nothing left to give, dig deeper and give a little more. It may sound clichéd but if you can dream it, you can do it.

Thoughts and recommendations
Tim Sharp

I've known Justine for quite a few years now. From the moment we met, I found her both likeable and inspirational. She's one of those people whose smile just lights up a room. This may well be (at least in part) attributable to the joy and satisfaction she gains from the wonderful work she (and her business) does.

I wasn't sure whether or not to include Justine's story in this book because, truth be told, she hasn't really experienced adversity or trauma in the way the other contributors have. But after much consideration I decided that wasn't really important. What I wanted to include in this book was a range of stories, in different voices, that different people could relate to. And I believe that many readers will relate to the early part of Justine's story that included almost intolerable occupational boredom.

How many of us go through life doing whatever we are doing just to pay the bills?

How many of us sacrifice or give up on our passions and dreams because we don't think pursuing them is realistic?

To live is the rarest thing in the world; most people exist, that is all.

This quote, attributed to Oscar Wilde, is one of my favourites. And it can be further strengthened by another famous quote from another famous person, Steve Jobs:

Your time is limited, so don't waste it living someone else's life. Don't be trapped by dogma, which is living with the results of other people's thinking. Don't let the noise of other's opinions drown out your own inner voice. And most important, have the courage to follow your heart and intuition. They somehow already know what you truly want to become. Everything else is secondary.

Justine shows us that we can live our very own lives and that we can pursue our dreams and make them real. Even more so, she shows us that in doing so, we can love our life as well as our work – and help other people love their lives along the way, too.

So although not as dramatic as some of the other challenges faced by some of the other authors in this book, I'm confident that Justine's experience of being 'trapped in the cold clutches of the corporate world where life was simply the repetition of a meaningless, unfulfilling cycle of events' is one that (sadly) many will find all too familiar.

But the good news is that Justine escaped this trap; and if she can do this and create something better, then why can't you?

This, I believe, is the most important lesson we can all take from Justine's impressive and inspiring story. We all have the choice to continue to follow the path expected or easiest, or we can take off along the road less travelled, which is frequently also the road most rewarding!

Making a decision like Justine made or achieving the success she has enjoyed is not easy. In fact, for a variety of reasons it may well be extremely difficult and possibly not even feasible for some. But difficult is not impossible; and even if you can't do all that

Justine has done, I'm sure there are some things you can do. Never underestimate the potential benefits that can come from doing small things, especially if you do them consistently!

So what can you take away and implement in your own life? How about trying the following:

- Reflect on what you'd be doing in your ideal life – what do you love? What are you passionate about? What energises you?
- What would it take for you to pursue this and make it a reality?
- Break these necessary actions down into small, manageable steps and make a plan that will help you move closer to this over a realistic time frame.
- Seek help from those who have expertise in areas that you're interested in.
- If you can't make your dreams a reality full time, can you follow your passion part time? Or can you bring your passion and energy and love into what you're already doing? Would it be possible to recraft your current job or career into something that's more enjoyable?
- Look long and don't give up. (Rome wasn't built in a day and Justine didn't create Inspired Adventures overnight.)
- Accept that life will not always be easy, but that we can cope when we focus on what really matters. Justine writes about how her daughter helped her stay present and mindful and that she also helped her appreciate the little things. So find that focus in your life. As Nietzsche once said, 'He who has a why to live can bear almost any how.'

Dr Happy

Tim Sharp

As I've been working on this book for the last year or so, I've been filled with admiration for the openness and honesty each of the contributors has shown in sharing the intimate details of their personal lives.

I came to conclude that if I've asked them to share their stories then maybe I should share at least some of my own.

If you asked me to describe how I feel about my current work as Dr Happy, the Chief Happiness Officer at The Happiness Institute, I would happily, and without qualification, note that I love what I do and am very proud of what I've achieved over the last few decades.

But I'd also like to respond to something you may well be thinking and to a question I'm frequently asked, which goes something like … 'Are you always happy?'

I always respond with a definite 'No!' because no-one is happy all the time. It would be unrealistic to expect to be happy all the time and, in fact, if someone tells me they're happy all the time, I'm actually somewhat concerned!

My response is an important attempt to ensure that people have realistic expectations of the sustainability of happiness, but it's also more than that. While I have no qualms acknowledging that I'm not happy all the time, I now want to add that I've definitely not been happy all my life. And there are still times when I'm markedly unhappy.

What I've not ever fully explained to anyone beyond my immediate family is that I have a history of depression. To this day I continue to struggle with depression, even though my life has immeasurably improved and even though I do all I can (mostly successfully) to take care of my psychological and physical health.

The fact is there have been periods in my life, most of which date back quite a few years, when I didn't want to live because I couldn't see a life worth living. There are still times when I struggle to manage the self-destructive and ridiculously self-critical demons that plague my mind from time to time. And for many years I used alcohol to self-medicate my depression, although I soon realised this was not helping long term.

Lana writes about curing herself of depression and anxiety, but the reality is that for most of us who've suffered depression or any other form of psychopathology, the struggle is ongoing. I'm pleased to say that for me it has undoubtedly become easier as I've mastered effective strategies and fundamentally changed certain ways I think about and live my life; but I still have periods of darkness that knock me down. Thankfully, I've become much better at picking myself up more quickly.

So I can relate to many of the stories in this book and I'm sure, because of what we know from the research into mental ill-health prevalence in our society today, that many of you probably can too!

So why have I not told this story before? I've asked myself this many times over the years and there are several answers I've always given.

In the early days, my silence mostly stemmed from a lack of understanding (and maturity) of the condition. I hardly understood what was going on myself, and what I did understand, I didn't have the vocabulary or courage to express to others. I was also very aware of the social stigma having depression attracted … and I didn't want anyone to think that of me. A few years later on, excited by and optimistic about my recovery, I thought talking about the past would not help and might even precipitate a relapse; something I obviously didn't want to experience.

As I began to establish my professional career as a clinical psychologist I was determined not to share my story, not so much now due to stigma or embarrassment, but more so because I wanted my skills and technical abilities to stand on their own. I wanted to be known as a competent therapist because of my qualifications and not because of my personal experience. Rightly or wrongly, at the time I didn't think this was important or right.

As I became more and more established as Dr Happy (and as I became happier and happier), I began to think it would be almost too clichéd to explain that I'd sought happiness because I'd previously been depressed! And to be perfectly honest, I also thought (and still believe to some extent) that no-one would care! Why would anyone be interested in my personal story? It's not as dramatic as many others; I wasn't famous in a way that made me of interest in that sense, and in almost every way I've lived a good and privileged life, so did I even deserve to be depressed in the first place?

As I read through these reasons for not talking publicly about my depression I ask myself if these are not just excuses, the same type of excuses I've encouraged others to overcome or put aside in the interests of smashing the stigma and helping others feel more confident to also speak out and get help. And the simple reality is that yes, they were and are excuses, but that doesn't mean they weren't valid or appropriate for me at that point in time. Timing is crucial when it comes to facing problems and especially when it comes to dealing with problems. In short, the time is now right for me.

The reasons I'm ready now are many and varied. To some extent I've reached a stage in life where I don't care so much about what others think. But mostly I've learnt, thanks to the wonderful people I've met throughout my life, that everyone's story is valid and worthwhile. You see, anyone's story can include episodes of depression or negative life events; and the negative life events need not be as dramatic as the traumas described in this book. But that doesn't make them any less disturbing or any less important. Far from it.

The reality is that there are probably far more people out there who've suffered depression (or some other form of psychological distress) as a result of negative reactions to normal life than have suffered the severe events experienced by some that gain the newspaper headlines. But again, that doesn't make any of them more or less important. As far as I'm concerned, what is important is that we can work through these situations, and what I hope this book achieves is the inspiration and motivation to do so.

I hope by finally telling my story that I might make it easier for even just one more person to feel comfortable telling their own story and to seek help. And just as importantly, I hope this helps my children, family and friends understand more about me, how I've worked hard to be happier and healthier, and how accordingly, anyone can lead a good life by determining what they need to do and making those to do's a non-negotiable part of their daily lives.

The wrap-up

I'm so proud of these amazing stories from a truly inspirational collection of individuals. It was both motivating and an incredible honour to comment on these stories for your reading and learning pleasure.

I do hope that you've been inspired by these chapters. I've highlighted issues in each that I believe to be important. In addition, I've done my best to provide relevant, practical tips and strategies you can put into practice in your own life. However, don't limit yourself to my suggestions; feel free to take anything you've learnt or been inspired to do and apply it in a way that works for you.

And that's the key to successful transformation ... it needs to work for you.

One of the reasons I pulled together this diverse range of stories is so that you can see there's not one path to take. Or if there is one path it's *your* path; the one that makes sense and works for you, the one that suits your strengths and fits your context.

As this book has shown, the right path might not necessarily be the first path. So keep trying; if you're going through hell, keep going. Don't give up and don't forget that you're never alone. There are always others, like Lana and Seb, like Joey and Justine, who are asking similar questions and facing similar obstacles.

Don't forget also that if they've survived and thrived, then you can too. Because with all due respect, these people are not superheroes! They're not necessarily even extraordinary! They might have achieved the extraordinary, but that has come about by simply doing the ordinary consistently and with perseverance; something I fervently and passionately believe we can *all* do.

And remember, you can't start the next chapter of your life if you keep re-reading the last one. So now that you've finished this book, it's time for you to go forward and live the rest of *your* amazing life!

About the contributors

Jean-Paul Bell has been described as one of Australia's great humour-manitarians. Since creating and co-founding the Humour Foundation and its Clown Doctor Program in 1996, Jean-Paul has been showing the world that laughter is the best medicine. In 2010 he published the book, *Laughter is the Best Medicine*, which chronicles the experiences of a number of clown doctors as they do their rounds at children's hospitals around Australia. Jean-Paul is also known for taking his physical comedy to war-torn countries like Afghanistan and East Timor, as shown on the ABC documentary *Honeymoon in Kabul*. Jean-Paul's great passions are health and education. Most recently he has been involved in The SMILE Study, a federally funded randomised trial with the Dementia Collaborative Research Centre at The University of NSW, visiting eighteen aged care homes to deliver fun and laughter to elderly people suffering with dementia. Jean-Paul has also spent 35 years working in theatre and education, performing for almost a million children. He teaches mime, movement and clowning to both teachers and children. He believes the performing arts are a great influence in child development, making children more confident, articulate and creative as they progress into their working lives. For more information go to artshealthinstitute.org.au

Sam Cawthorn is the CEO for SpeakersInstitute.com.au, a company dedicated to advancing humanity by helping the next generation of speaking talent get their message out into the world. He is an accomplished author, having written six books including an international bestseller. He is also a philanthropist who has started a charity working with kids living with a disability in developing worlds. Sam is the 2015 Entrepreneur of the Year and also the Young Australian of the Year. Sam has a diverse background within the Australian Federal Government as a Youth Futurist and is also a highly skilled musician, and one of the only people in the world that plays the guitar with an above elbow amputation. He also brags about having the most advanced bionic arm in the world, which he programs with his iPhone 5S. Sam's passion stretches as far as India where he has set up his own charity. For more information go to samcawthorn.com

Justine Curtis believes in living life to the full, experiencing the world and encouraging others to make a difference to people's lives. Her belief in the power of volunteering, community work and supporting others in any form is the cornerstone of her business philosophy. Having worked in corporate and not-for-profit direct marketing for over a decade, Justine created Inspired Adventures following her own challenging ascent of Mount Kilimanjaro in 2004. Since then, Inspired Adventures has developed and managed over 320 adventures, each raising an average of $100,000 for charity partners. This year, Inspired Adventures will exceed $20 million fundraised for charity. Some of Justine's most memorable Inspired Adventure moments include: camping high in the Himalayas; seeing Machu Picchu for the first time; trekking the Great Wall of China along the Mongolian border; camel-riding through the Rajasthan desert; and trekking through the highest tea plantations in the world. Justine has a beautiful (and very well-travelled) six-year-old daughter Indigo (Indi). Indi has accompanied Justine to India, Bhutan, the US and New Zealand (just to name a few). Justine says Indi is her life's greatest adventure and a constant source of inspiration. For more go to inspiredadventures.com.au.

Dr Maggie Haertsch is a co-founder, executive director and CEO of the Arts Health Institute. She is also the editor in chief of *Spoonful*, an arts in health magazine, and a producer with Hot Tin Productions. With over 30 years' experience in the healthcare industry, Maggie began her career as a registered nurse and midwife. She holds a PhD in Behavioural Sciences in Medicine and has worked in a number of academic, teaching and research positions. As a producer she has film credits for documentaries including *The Smile Within* and *Stumbling in Hillary's Footsteps*. Maggie has undertaken roles as a health consultant in East Timor and remote areas of Australia. She has business experience in Australia, the UK and USA and is the recipient of a number of awards, including Enterprise Woman of the Year and PricewaterhouseCoopers X-Factor award for best innovation contribution to Australian industry. For more information go to artshealthinstitute.org.au

Petrea King is the CEO of the Quest for Life Foundation, which she established in 1989. She is a frequent keynote speaker at medical and other conferences, a facilitator, teacher and trainer and, for the past fifteen years, has been a monthly guest on ABC radio's *Midweek Conference* and *Nightlife* where she discusses the challenges of living a meaningful life in the midst of challenging circumstances. Petrea has received the Advance Australia Award, Citizen of the Year and the Centenary Medal for her contribution to the community and has been nominated for Australian of the Year each year since 2003 as well as being a NSW finalist for Senior Australian of the Year in 2011. In 2003 she was celebrated on Channel 9's *This Is Your Life* and has been featured in *Australian Story*, *Compass* and many other television and radio productions. Petrea lives very happily with her partner Wendie Batho, two rescue cattle dogs Meg and Maxi, and four Welsummer chickens in Bundanoon, NSW.

Petrea holds qualifications as a naturopath, herbalist, clinical hypnotherapist, yoga and meditation teacher and is a bestselling author of eight books and a dozen meditation practices available through iTunes or on CD from www.questforlife.com.au.

Cynthia Morton is a skilled specialist in the field of emotional fitness. Her workshops, lectures and private sessions offer a unique, gentle yet disarming approach to wounded hearts in need of understanding and solutions. Through the art of heartfelt storytelling both on the page and on the stage Cynthia is often described as delivering a powerful wake-up call. Shedding a helpful light on the darker side of the human heart, she emotionally disrobes without a trace of shame. She reveals challenging life lessons learnt while recovering from her own issues of childhood abuse, violence, suicide, addiction, bankruptcy, smother mothering and divorce. The Emotional Fitness approach to life Cynthia explains often involves 'disturbing the comfortable and comforting the disturbed'. Cynthia's free Daily Word Vitamins and videos are accessible at Balancebydeborahhutton.com and at cynthiamorton.com. Her Weekly Word Vitamin videos and blogs are available at www.stylemagazines.com. Alternatively follow her on Twitter @cynthiajmorton or Facebook to receive updates. If you would like to find out more about Emotional Fitness private personal training sessions and working one on one with Cynthia, please email her directly on: cynthia@emotionalfitness.com.

Lana Penrose is the bestselling author of *To Hellas and Back*, *Kickstart My Heart*, *Addicted to Love* and *The Happiness Quest*. Lana has appeared on national breakfast television and multiple radio programs, and her books have featured in *Vogue, Cleo, Famous, Woman's Day, That's Life* and countless metropolitan and broadsheet newspapers. She has appeared as a guest speaker on four panels at the prestigious Byron Bay Writers' Festival and has spoken at the Mind and its Potential conference. Prior to becoming a published author, Lana worked in the entertainment industry for various record companies, music publications, television (including MTV), Simon Cowell and Darren Hayes of Savage Garden. Today she is a qualified counsellor and volunteers as a crisis support worker with Lifeline and as a speaker for beyondblue. To discover more about Lana and her work, please feel free to visit: www.lanapenrose.com.au.

Ingrid Poulson has been speaking about and training in resilience and positive living to a diverse and expansive audience since 2006. Ingrid has completed degrees in Arts, Education and Cognitive Science and her book, *Rise*, was released in 2008 by Macmillan Australia, quickly becoming the number one selling non-fiction book. Ingrid is a highly experienced facilitator and trainer and combines her academic background with her uniquely qualified life experience to build resilience in others. Ingrid now relishes her life with her husband and two young children on the South Coast of NSW.

Sebastian Robertson founded the social enterprise Batyr in 2011 and was its founding CEO for almost five years. Batyr has become a national leader in innovative programs, focusing on the engagement and education of youth in mental health. Sebastian is now the managing director of a private renewable energy company that focuses on exploring and enhancing energy efficiency for businesses and consumers. He sits on the Board of Batyr as well as James and Co, an ethical clothing label, and has experience in leadership positions at a national level. Sebastian complements his experience in social innovation and enterprise with a double degree in Economics and Commerce and prior to establishing Batyr worked for General Electric, a top ten Forbes Global 2000 Company. In 2011 he was named Sydney Social Entrepreneur of the Year by the School for Social Entrepreneurs and in 2013 was recognised by his alma mater as Young Alumnus of the Year at the Australian National University. He has a passion for bringing sustainable business models to key societal issues and loves to explore innovative ways to engage and educate those around him. Despite what you may be thinking about his resume, he insists that his good fortune has come from being able to recognise and surround himself with incredible people who continue to inspire him on a daily basis while he focuses on providing the light entertainment. For more information go to www.batyr.com.au.

Allan Sparks is a corporate speaker and published author. His book *The Cost of Bravery* was published by Penguin Books Australia in 2013 and reprinted in 2015. Allan also spends much of his time helping others. He is a beyondblue ambassador, a Soldier On ambassador and a member of the National Leadership Group of Suicide Prevention Australia. He volunteers to travel the country, sharing his experiences. He gives hope of recovery to others and helps break down the stigma of mental illness. You can connect with Allan on twitter @allansparkes and Linkedin. Find out more about him on his website www.allansparkes.com and his facebook page facebook.com/AllanSparkesCV.

Sam Webb was born in Sydney in 1988 but spent most of his earlier years on Queensland's Gold Coast. Sam relocated to Sydney in 2014 after pursuing an acting career and being accepted in to one of Sydney's most prestigious acting schools, Screenwise. Sam has featured on a number of TV commercials and was also one of the contestants on Fox Sports *Maximus Academy*, Series 2. Outside of acting, Sam spends a lot of his time training, and was recently awarded a scholarship to the Australian Institute of Fitness where he will be studying his Master Trainer. Sam is the co-founder and CEO of the registered charity organisation LIVIN. Along with his best friend Casey Lyons, LIVIN created a fashion line that promotes the message 'It ain't weak to speak' to get people talking about mental illness. Find out more at livin.org.au.

Joe Williams is a proud Wiradjuri Aboriginal man born in Cowra, and raised in Wagga NSW. Joe played National Rugby League before switching to professional boxing in 2009. He is the current two times WBF World Jnr Welterweight champion and WBC Asia Continental champion. Joe also dedicates his time to motivational speaking across the country, addressing all things motivation, resilience and living a highly successful life while managing severe mental illness. Joe can be contacted at joewilliams.com.au.